W. L. Fosdick

My voyage around the globe

W. L. Fosdick

My voyage around the globe

ISBN/EAN: 9783744737500

Printed in Europe, USA, Canada, Australia, Japan

Cover: Foto ©Andreas Hilbeck / pixelio.de

More available books at **www.hansebooks.com**

MY VOYAGE

AROUND THE GLOBE.

BY W. L. FOSDICK.

Portraying life on the Ocean as it was sixty years ago. Interesting and instructive reminiscences of travel and adventure on land and sea, extending over a period of seven and one-half years, including a description of whaling, and the experiences of three years spent with the natives of the South Pacific.

"The sea! the sea! the open sea,
The blue, the fresh, the ever free!
Without a mark, without a bound,
It runneth the earth's wide regions round.
It plays with the clouds; it mocks the skies;
Or like a cradled creature lies."
—BARRY CORNWALL.

SHAWANO, WIS.,
WIEGAND & ESSER, PRINTERS,
1897.

DEDICATION.

To gratify the wishes of my Children and Grandchildren this work was undertaken; and to them it is affectionately dedicated, by THE AUTHOR.

PREFACE.

WHEN I began writing the sketches of my early life embodied in this volume, I did not intend them for publication. At the request of my children and grandchildren, I undertook to prepare for them a simple narrative of my travels on land and sea, without the embellishments of the book-maker's art. Simply something they could read and keep in remembrance of me and as a relic of my boyhood days.

But as I continued to write until my manuscript assumed considerable proportions, my family and friends persuaded me to re-write the whole and put it in shape for the press. The result is herewith submitted to the consideration of the reading public.

This book is a faithful record of my personal experience and observation, and if he who reads for information shall feel himself repaid when he has finished its pages, I shall deem that my best reward.

It is a great source of pleasure and satisfaction to me to have seen the wonders of nature, and to know that God in his providence has provided for the sustenance of his children of every race and degree, high and low, in every land and clime. W. L. FOSDICK.

Shawano, Wis., January 20, 1897.

My Voyage Around the Globe.

CHAPTER I.

FROM LAKE COUNTY TO THE EQUATOR.

Opening scenes—A friend at Albany—The whaleship Margaret Scott—Capt. Plaskett, the "Old Horse"—The start from New Bedford—Making Marline—Purpoise fishing—Flying fish—Sailors' laws—Cape de Verde Islands—Capt. Plaskett has tremens—Crossing the equator—Neptune initiates a subject—Incidents and anecdotes.

I was born in the northern part of the state of New York, in the year 1823. The following year my parents removed to Lake county, Ohio. Here my mother died when I was about seven years of age, and my father followed her about seven years later.

The following year, at the age of fifteen, I had determined to see more of the planet on which we live, and prepared to go to sea. My guardian, Benjamin Blish by name, and a very worthy gentleman, tried to persuade me to remain at school. Friends joined him in the effort to overcome resolution by portraying the dangers and hardships of a seaman's life. But I had made up my mind to see something of the other side of the world.

In conversation with a gentleman by the name of Packard, I had made my wishes known. He had formerly resided at Nantucket, a great whaling port at the time of which I write. He wrote to some ship owners for me. In reply they stated that they had several fine ships fitting out for sea, wanted men and boys and could give me a berth. My uncle was captain of a vessel on Lake Erie and

I had passage with him from Lake county to Buffalo, N. Y. He tried to dissuade me from my purpose, but my mind was unalterably fixed and I continued my journey, via the Erie canal to Albany.

While crossing a drawbridge at the latter place, an old Englishman who attended the draw and run a little peanut stand, hailed me and the following dialogue ensued:

"My lad, where are you going?"

"I am going on a whaling voyage."

"Where are you from?"

"Ohio."

"What part of the state?"

"Fairport."

"What is your name?"

"Fosdick."

"What! Colonel Fosdick's son?"

"Yes, sir."

"I knew your father well."

He took an interest in me at once, and finally said: "If you are short of money, I will get a man to take charge of you; you will not have to pay anything until you are on board of a ship, then it will be charged to you and deducted from your wages." I thought that would be all right. He went on board the steamer Knickerbocker with me and talked with one of the officers who took me in charge. At 4 o'clock p. m. we were under way en route for New York where we arrived the following morning at 9 o'clock.

The officer went with me across the city to where the shipping offices were located on the East River side, a distance of about three miles from where the steamer landed. Above the door of the office we entered, a strip of canvass was stretched displaying the picture of a whale and the words, "Whalemen Wanted." The officer talked with the man at the desk, received some money (my fare on the steamer I presume) and went away. The man then asked my name, and when I told him replied: "That is my name, we are connected, and I know several mariners by the name of Fosdick." The office was nicely fitted up including a fine library. He directed me to a place on Cherry street where I could board until he had secured more men, then we would proceed to New Bedford. About four weeks later, in company with eleven others, I was sent on to New Bedford. The steamer Washington took us as far as Stonington, R. I., when we took the cars and finished the journey by rail. We found them engaged in coppering the bottom of our vessel, and we staid at a boarding house six weeks before she was ready for sea. She was a four boat ship fitted out for a four years' voyage.

The ship was named Margaret Scott, after the wife of General Winfield Scott, and the figurehead was a life-like representation of the head and bust of that lady. Splendid life-size portraits of General Scott and wife reclining under a canopy composed of American flags and the national coat of arms adorned the stern.

The captain, William Plaskett, was a rough, drinking man, but his reputation as a lucky whaleman always secured him a ship. He would walk around in the shipping office and, in the hearing of sailors, would say to Mr. Parkhurst, one of the owners: "I want you to ship me good men, for I am a horse!"—"Hell afloat," and other remarks of like import. Among those who heard him were six sailors who made up their minds to ship with him and arrange a little program for his benefit. When all the details of fitting had been completed and the ship had hauled out into the Bay ready for the start, these men came alongside in a boat by themselves. One of them climbed onto the deck and the others passed him a number of articles not ound in the catalogue of a whaleman's outfit. These inc'uded a saddle; a bridle; a pair of spurs; a heavy whip and a bundle of hay. The captain was walking on the quarter deck at the time, in company with the pilot and officers. When his eye caught the layout piled on deck, he stopped short and viewed it with astonishment. "What do you mean by bringing that rigging on board ship?" he demanded. One of the men stepped forward and said: "We heard you say you are a horse;—we intend to do our duty as men, and if you do not do yours as master of the ship, we will saddle you, put the bits in your mouth, ride you with whip and spur, and feed you on that bundle of hay." When I say that Capt. Plaskett was angry, I put it mild, but he had to swallow his wrath and content himself with ordering them to go ashore, declaring that he would not go to sea with such men. Of course, they expected this and went willingly. We were delayed two days getting men to fill their places.

When the ship's company was complete there were forty-three persons on board. The crew numbered thirty-two, and the passenger list eleven, to wit: A carpenter and his wife, bound for the island of Tahiti, one of the Society group; four Mormon missionaries, bound for South Pacific points, and a Dr. Winslow, wife, two children and servant girl, bound for the island of Mauee, one of the Hawaiian group, to take charge of a hospital under government appointment.

It was on the 6th day of October, 1838, that we sailed. We soon left the headlands of Buzzards Bay astern, the broad Atlantic with its mysteries, its dangers and attractions lay before us, and our good ship made obeisance to Neptune as she felt the heavy ground swell of old ocean.

This was the first voyage to several of the crew and they were seasick. The passengers succumbed to the inevitable and did not show themselves for nearly a week. The second day out we saw a large whaleship on the wind, homeward bound. She looked grand with all sail spread to the breeze. Some of our men would have given most anything to have been on board of her. Seasickness had resulted into homesickness, but they had to stand it. After crossing the gulf stream, we ran into fine weather. The green hands had recovered from seasickness, were getting their "sea legs" on, and everything began to move ship shape.

When we had been out three weeks, we had become acquainted with each other. Parley B. Pratt, one of the missionaries, was a very good story teller and liked to mingle with the sailors Another of these missionaries was nearly dead with consumption when he came on board at New Bedford and when we had been out about four weeks, he died Farther on, in portraying the details of a sailor's life, I include a description of a burial at sea and will omit it here.

We, the new hands, had learned some sailor phrases; could box the compass; steer our trick at the wheel; tie some of the sailor knots; go up the ratlines in seaman-like style, and began to consider ourselves "old salts". When not engaged in attending to the regular routine of ship duty, we were kept busy unlaying old standing rigging, i.e., pull out the rope yarns, knot them together and wind them in balls, preparatory to making spun yarn or marline. The marline is made by twisting three strands of rope yarn together with a contrivance called a wench. This consists of a long wooden spindle with an iron hook at the outer end, driven by a balance wheel attached to the windlass bits. One man turns the wench and one man attends to the twisting, rubbing the marline with a piece of tarred parsling as he spins. The marline is used for baling the whalebone: seizing and serving the rigging, etc. Then we had sails to mend, chafing gear to put on, etc. In short, plenty of work first, last, and all the time. A certain old lady once said to me: "La, sakes! I thought sailors had nothing to do but sit down and let the wind blow 'em around." Others may entertain the same idea but it is a mistake.

One day as we were nearing the Cape Verde islands, with a stiff breeze on our starboard quarter, we saw a school of porpoises making for the ship. They love to play in the foam and spray under the bows, and tumble in the billows rolled up by a ship when she is sailing fast. But indulgence in this pastime often costs a porpoise his life. A man goes out on the martingale guys with a sort of spear called a grains, consisting of one tine with a jointed flange, or beard that opens after it is thrust into the fish and holds him firmly impaled until landed on deck. The pan of the lower jaw contains a fatty substance that yields nearly its bulk in oil of very superior quality. for lubricating delicate machinery such as watches, clocks, etc. The flesh hashed with pork makes very good eating, and is sometimes used.

Schools of flying fish are seen frequently in these seas. They usually appear shooting out from the crest of a wave, and do not seem to be able to rise readily from the flat surface of the water during a calm. Their flight induced by the appearance of some enemy, no doubt, is short, seldom exceeding ten rods, if not carried farther by the wind. They are sometimes blown on board ship. We caught two in this way. The wings make nice book marks.

On board ship sailors have laws of their own that are rigidly enforced. A little incident in point occurred about this time. It is the rule for every man to leave his chest unlocked while out at sea, and woe to the man caught stealing from his shipmates. A number of us had missed certain articles and laid it to a big Irish Canadian. We appointed a man to search. First the chests were overhauled without success. Then we began to search the persons and when we came to the Canadian he objected, but we held him and found two stolen knives. A search of his bedding and mattress disclosed two shirts, a revolver and some other small articles. He might better have gone to prison. Every sailor was down on him. He hardly dared open his mouth—got a slap in the face whenever he did. They abused him with kicks and cuffs, and the first port we made he was put ashore.

"Land, ho!" rang out from the masthead. We had been out six weeks, and this was the first time we had heard this call. The land in sight was the Island of St Nicholas, one of the Cape de Verde group. We approached the shore and laid off and on. One small boat went ashore with the captain, and the doctor and his wife. They hired donkeys and rode out into the country to see the sights. Returning in the evening they brought some oranges and bananas, and the sailors brought some stone bottles filled with cocoanut rum, called by the Portugese "angadent." It caused quite a riot among the officers and sailors. We sailed that night, and the next morning found ourselves off St. Jago, a larger island of the same group. We went ashore with the passengers. This time the captain picked a new boats' crew that he thought would not be so likely to buy rum. I was one of those selected. The population appeared to be largely composed of mixed Portugese and negro blood, only partially civilized. Children entirely nude, some of them as old as twelve or fourteen years were playing in the sand. I think our lady passengers were somewhat embarrassed. We staid about six hours and set sail.

Our Captain was about the hardest looking specimen of humanity I have ever seen. Dark, swarthy complexion and voice like a roaring lion. He had six barrels of New England rum in the run under the cabin, and was "full" most of the time. The sailors had no love for him.

Christmas day we were near the equator and the weather was very hot. We had sprung our main topmast and were engaged in the work of sending up a new one. "Old horse," as the sailors called him, stood looking up and bellowing at the men. All of a sudden he dropped as though he had been shot. Didn't even have to say: "I've got 'em!" but that was what was the matter. He had the tremens. He was carried into the cabin and Dr. Winslow thought he would die, but in less than three weeks he was on deck again to the evident disappointment of the sailors.

About this time I had my first experience with toothache. The mate told me the captain had a pair of turnkeys to pull teeth, and I had better go to him. I ventured to approach him and say: "Captain, could you pull a tooth for me?" "Yes," he thundered, "pull every d—d tooth in your head!" It frightened me so that I did not have toothache again for a week, then I got Mr. Rogers, one of the missionaries, to pull it for me.

As we approached the line, the passengers began to talk among themselves, wondering if old Neptune would make us a visit. The second mate overheard them and told them that, as the crew included a number of new subjects, it would be Neptune's duty to come on board and initiate them into the mysteries of a seaman's life, where we touched the equator. All were anxious to witness the services, could think of nothing but Neptune's prospective visit, and were constantly on the lookout for him.

At last their long, tedious watch was abruptly terminated. A heavy voice rising apparently from the ocean, shouted: "Ship, ahoy! What ship is this?" The second mate replied: "The Margaret Scott." "Are there any subjects on board for Neptune?" "Yes, we have one." "Then prepare for the services." And Neptune appeared above the night-head, speaking trumpet in hand, and stepped upon the deck. He was about six feet in hight, with broad shoulders and a gruff voice. A mat of rope yarns enveloped him from waist to feet, and a fringe of same hung from collar to waist. A light duck mask painted red, with black mustache, whiskers and eyebrows, covered his face. Above this towered a tall cap, bearing the word, "Neptune." His belt held a cutlass, and the speaking trumpet after he had reached the deck. Clad in such paraphernalia, he was a horrible looking object, well calculated to strike terror to the hearts of the uninitiated, as he displayed his razor (piece of hoop-iron) and mug (bucket of "slush").

The cannon was dismounted without delay, Neptune seated himself upon the carriage and was drawn aft to the main hatch by six sturdy sailors.

The program had been arranged on the quiet, for fun, and the amusement of the passengers. Formerly, subjects were often put through dangerous ordeals, and keel-hauling sometimes resulted in drowning; but now the naval laws forbade doing anything to injure the person.

The victim selected in this instance was a boy about twenty years of age, not very bright but stubborn and fearless. He made a good subject. It took two good men to hold him after his legs were bound. There were so many new hands on board, it is quite likely there would have been a row if they had selected any of us beside this one. A little incident that occurred about this time will serve to illustrate his characteristics:

On shipboard, the regular ration of molasses is one quart to each man, once a week, sufficient to sweeten his coffee and dress his duff. This boy had a weakness for cane juice, would crumb bread into his allowance as soon as it was dealt out, eat it like so much bread and milk, then improve every opportunity to filch it from the others. We concluded to satisfy his craving for once, at least. So one day when he had received and stowed away his own, as usual, a delegation took him in hand and compelled him to continue his feast. A second quart followed the first with neatness and dispatch; but the old saying, "two is company, three is a crowd," applied in this case, and only a portion of the third quart had gone to the bourne, from whence all subsequently returned. where there was unmistakable evidence of internal strife. At this juncture the mate appeared on the scene, terminated the compulsory repast, and made the victim drink a pint of salt water. The action of the emetic was prompt and emphatic, the boy rushed to the rail and dumped his troubles into the sea. The one treatment effected a lasting cure. Keeley has hardly parallelled this record of overcoming a morbid appetite. He never so much as called for his own allowance of molasses afterward.

All was now ready, and Neptune called for his subject. He was at the wheel, but was immediately relieved and brought before the master of ceremonies, who catechised as follows:

"What is your name?"

"Washington Enos Cune, from Vairmount state."

"Do you use tobacco, or drink rum?"

"No."

"What is an ordinary seaman's duty?"

"Hand, reef and steer."

"What is it to hand a sail?"

"Furl it."

"Name the reefs in the topsail."

"Single reef, double reef and close reef."

"Can you box the compass from north to south?"

"I will try: North; north by east; north northeast; northeast by north; northeast; northeast by east; east northeast; east by north; east; east by south; east southeast; southeast by east; southeast; southeast by south; south southeast; south by east; south."

"You save one shave by answering correctly. I will try you on able seamen's duty."

"How would you commence to reef topsails?"

"Lower away the yard on the cap, haul up the reef tackle, bringing the leech of the sail up to the yard, lift the dog's ear, pass the earing, haul to leeward and knot away."

"What are the names of the sails on the mainmast?"

"Mainsail, topsail, top gallant sail, royal and skysail."

"I see you will have to be shaved." To the sailors in charge of the subject: "Put the canvas around his neck, I will make a full fledged sailor of him." And he proceeded to use the brush.

"Keep it out of my mouth!"

"Quiet, quiet, my lad! This is only the first lather, I must put some on the upper part of your jawbone."

"Keep it out of my eyes!"

"Shut your eyes. You must commit to memory what I tell you. Hold his arms! My knife is not sharp, but I must shave close to take off the shore dust."

"Keep that brush out of my mouth!"

'Steady, boy, keep anchored or you may lose your eyebrows. It takes lots of slush to shave this fellow, but he will make a good seaman when I get through with him. Now repeat after me the names of the sails on the mainmast: After the skysail comes the moon sail, stargazer, skyscraper and the heavenly peeper. Now do you think you can remember? These are sails, but you will never see them set."

"There are others on board who never crossed the equator before; why don't you shave them?"

"We shall shave some of them some dark night. Some will never make sailors and will be put ashore the first port we enter. Now, men, take this subject forward and wash him up. He will not fear to cross the equator hereafter."

CHAPTER II.

WHALE FISHING.

Preparatory arrangements aboard ship—The pursuit and capture of leviathan—Dangers of the chase—Securing and stowing the oil and bone—Death of our first mate—St. Paul's Island—Captain and new mate have a row—Trouble between the captain and Dr. Winslow—Island of Toboai—Arrive at Tabiti.

We had now entered upon the South Atlantic whaling grounds, and when we reached a point a few degrees south of the Tristan d' Acunha Islands, began our work.

Before proceeding to relate our experiences in the chase of leviathan, I will describe and explain some things that may interest the reader and enable him to better understand what follows.

Each man gets his board and a certain share of oil and bone, according to his experience as a sailor, or whaleman. This share, called a "lay", constitutes his only compensation for services and is lucrative in proportion to the success of the voyage. If the ship returns with a full cargo, he has a good sum to his credit when he settles up.

There are four mates, each has command of a boat when in chase of the whale, and when acting in this capacity is called boatheader, and it is part of his duty to lance the whale. The harpooner, always an experienced seaman, throws the harpoons and makes fast to the whale.

The boats are twenty-six feet in length, built of light material, bow and stern shaped alike that they may be backed or shoved astern when necessary, as easily as they can be propelled ahead. And it is always necessary to back away as soon as the whale feels iron, and the best time the whalemen can make is none too quick. The oarlocks are muffled that they may approach the gigantic prey without noise. Sockets in the bottom of the boat hold the oars apeak when the men are attending to other duties. When in fair striking distance, the harpooner, standing in the bows, throws the barbed harpoons and they plunge deep into the monster's side.

Six men constitutes a boat's crew, always; every man handles an oar; each oar has a name, to-wit: Harpooneer oar, bow oar, midship oar, tub oar, after oar and steering oar.

In the bows are two harpoons, two lances, and a hatchet and knife to cut the line in case of accident. In the stern are kept a compass, a lantern, six sperm candles, a keg of sea bread and sometimes an extra keg of water. Some carry a quadrant to assist in calculating latitude in case the boat should get lost from the ship.

In the after part of the boat are a large and a small tub holding the whale lines. The lines are made of best manilla and are prepared and coiled in the tubs before they are placed in the boats in the following manner: A line with a heavy billet of wood attached is towed astern of the ship from twelve to twenty-four hours. It is then handed on board and dried, then passed over a block aloft, brought down and coiled into the tubs back-handed. Beginning at the outside, the line is coiled snug and smooth to the centre carried straight across to the outside again and the process repeated until the tubs are full. The two hold about one hundred and fifty fathoms of line. That in the large tub is run out first and the reserve line in the small tub bent on, if necessary. Sometimes the entire length is insufficient, when the whale sounds unusually deep or makes straight away until it becomes necessary to cut loose to save the boat and crew.

The care taken in preparing and coiling the line, as above described, is necessary to make sure that it will pay out without kinking.

When a whale is sighted and the boat is ready for the start, the exposed end of the line is lifted from the large tub, passed with a turn or two around a post in the stern, called a loggerhead, carried forward over the oars to the bow, passed through a groove or chock lined with zinc or lead, brought back to the right a little and bent onto the harpoons.

There are several species of whale to-wit: The sperm whale, the black or right whale, the fin-backed, the humpbacked and the sulphur bottom. The first two are the kind sought. The others do not yield oil enough to pay, and the two last named are found mostly in bays aud inlets. The black fish is the smallest of the whale species and yields from three to five barrels of oil. The sperm whale has but one spout and blows ahead. The right whale has two and sprays right and left. The black or right whale is found mostly in high latitudes both north and south, its particular haunts being determined by the presence of "britt" upon which it feeds. The sperm whale is found in the temperate and torrid zones, is provided with teeth and feeds upon squid and fish. The sperm whale's defense is his head, the right whale defends with his flukes.

Two men are kept aloft on the top gallant crosstrees, fore and main, on lookout for whale, and are relieved every two hours. When a whale appears on the surface or spouts, the man that describes it sings out:

"There she blows!"

"Where away?"

"Two points off the starboard bow."

"What does she look like?

"Right whale."

There is great excitement when a whale is sighted, in getting the boats ready for the start. The preliminaries are quickly disposed of and at the order "lower away" the boat is let over the side by means of the davitt tackles with two men in it ready to unhook the minute she touches the water. It requires tact to get down the ship's side into the boat, as the ship is rolling and the boat setting away into the trough of the sea. Sometimes you may step off the chains thinking you have but a short step and drop eight or ten feet into the bottom of the boat. You have to watch your chance and step quick.

Now the boats are off after the whale, and during their absence the ship is managed by the carpenter or boatbuilder, cooper, blacksmith, steward, cook and cabin boy. One man is sent aloft with a waif—a piece of painted cloth drawn over a hoop with a long handle attached, to "waif" or signal the direction of the whale to the boats. From his point of vantage he can see farther than the men in the boats. The men pull with a will and the boats fairly fly. The boat-header encouraging them with promises of new suits, houses and lots, etc. You can tell by the expression of his face when the monster is near. A moment later you can hear the whale spouting and feeding, then the command: "Stand up." The harpooneer peaks his oar, grabs the harpoons, throws them in quick succession, and sings out: "Stern all!" The whale sounds or goes down at a lively rate. The officers change places and the mate uses the lance. They hold on the line as it goes around the loggerhead.

The whale stays under water from fifteen to forty-five minutes, and when he reappears above the surface starts off at a terrific speed, lashing the sea furiously with his flukes, the blows resounding like claps of thunder. It is said they go at the rate of forty miles an hour. The men peak their oars, turn on the thwarts and haul line to overtake the prey. No attempt is made to recoil the line and it is dropped and towed astern as they advance. At the proper point the men return to the oars and pull for the monster's side, taking care to keep out of his sight and away from his flukes. The heart or "life" lies just back of the pectoral fin, and the lance must reach it to kill. When the boat gains the proper position, the mate uses the lance, and if he strikes the vital point the whale begins to spout blood; then the boat must get away quick for he is terrible in his "flurry" or death throes. It is lively work from first to last and frought with great danger.

Now the monster ceases to struggle, life is extinct and he rolls inertly with the motion of the waves. The prize is now towed alongside the ship meanwhile working up to meet the boats. He is secured by two heavy chains, one passed around the flukes and one hooked onto the fin. Heavy tackles running to the mainmast head, thence forward to the windlass are provided for hoisting. The head is disposed of first. If it is black or right whale only the upper part of the head is brought on deck. This contains the black whale bone of commerce, which is set in the gums in slabs varying in length from one to twelve feet by eight to ten inches in width, averaging about one inch in thickness at the base, and tapering to a point. The outer edge of these slabs are nearly straight and the inside edges are fringed like a horse's main, forming a perfect mat that catches the "brit." The whale swims with his mouth open when feeding, closing the enormous trap at intervals to blow the water out through his nostrils, and to suck down and swallow the accumulations of "brit." An individual "brit" is about the size and color of a grain of flax-seed

If it is a sperm whale, the whale head is usually hoisted on deck. The teeth are ivory of fine quality, and the cranium yields three to five barrels of oil, called case oil which constitutes the highest grade, and is obtained after the head is opened by simply bailing out, and requires no further treatment to prepare it for use.

The head disposed of, the next thing in order is to secure the blubber Provided with sharp, long handled spades, men are let over the side on stagings and further secured in their positions by breast mats attached to the side of the ship, cut the blubber in pieces about four feet wide and seven or eight in length, called blanket pieces. Beginning at, and including the fin in the first piece, they cut and peel, men on deck hoisting and rolling the whale as they proceed, until the piece is long enough, then a hole is cut a little below where it is severed, the bight of the rope from the second tackle is passed through and secured to what will be the second piece, the first is hauled on board and lowered into the hold. This is repeated, the men cutting round and round the whale spirally down to the flukes, when the carcass is cut adrift.

In the hold two men, one with a pike the other with a knife, lean the blanket pieces, i. e. remove any pieces of flesh that may be found adhering to the blubber, and cut it in pieces of convenient size, say six inches by twelve, called "horse" pieces, and pikes them on deck where a third man catches them with a hook, throws them onto a horse and holds them while a fourth man with a long knife that is provided with a handle at each end, slices it up and shoves it into a large tub ready for the kettles. Of these there are two of large size, set in brick arches, supported by iron knees bolted to the timbers of the deck. As the process of frying out progresses, the oil is bailed into a copper cooler, and the kettles replenished with the prepared blubber in the tubs. The cooling recepticle referred to is about three feet square by six feet in height, and is provided with a faucet near the top. To this faucet a hose is attached that conducts the partially cooled oil as it rises to a cask on deck. When cold, it is carried below by another hose to casks in the ground tier of the hold. Wood is used for the first fire and scraps are utilized to keep it going and makes a very hot fire. The bone is split out of the jaws with axes, packed in bales of five slabs each, bound with spun yarn or marlin and stowed between decks.

The sperm whale frequently makes a most determined resistance, and apparantly actuated by revenge, attempts to seize and destroy the boat with his jaws. The right whale will sweep its flukes through the air, bring them down suddenly on a boat, cut it asunder, killing some and hurling others stunned and bleeding a great distance. A yet more appalling calamity occasionally befalls an entire boat's crew,—the whale sounds perpendicular, the line gets foul of something in the boat, will not run out freely, and in the twinkling of an eye boat, crew and all are dragged down into the ocean.

When pulling onto a whale, the boatheader holds the steering oar and watches the game. He will not allow the men to look forward, for some have been known to become panic stricken at sight of the monster when near at hand, and jump out of the boat rather than run the chances of going nearer. The terrific noise and awful appearance of the leviathan is enough to frighten anyone but an old whaleman.

One day we captured a small black whale. or "calf." These are sometimes killed with the harpoons, and our harpooneer succeeded in reaching the vitals in this instance. The stricken whale spouted blood at once, his flukes sank limply into the sea, and he raised his head above the surface and groaned, or bellowed equal to the heaviest clap of thunder I ever heard, it fairly made the boat tremble. This one only yielded forty barrels of oil.

A sad accident resulting in the death of our first mate happened when we were in forty-five south latitude and at a point southeast of the Tristan Islands. We sighted a large right whale off our starboard beam and about two miles distance. We judged that he would have yielded four hundred barrels of oil if we had succeeded in killing him.

Three boats lowered and pulled after him. The mate's boat did not lower, but took what is called "ship's chance," that is the chance that the whale will dive before the other boats get in striking distance and come up between them and the ship, which was just what happened in this instance. He came up within half a mile of the ship.

I belonged to the mate's boat, and as soon as the whale reappeared, the orders: "Main yard aback and lower away! Give away men!" were given. We went onto him and put both harpoons into him. He sounded, came up and made off in the direction of the other floats. The second mate fastened to him, and then we knew there would be fun, strife for the honor of killing the whale, as a record is kept in the ship's journal and is a good recommend for the officer who secures the most prizes.

There is danger of getting stove when two boats are trying to use the lance. In their eagerness and excitement caution is forgotten. We went up to him on the right side and the mate was lancing him and saying: "Hold her up, boys, I'll fix him!" I was pulling the midship oar and saw that the monster was drawing ahead, every sweep of his flukes brought him nearer the boat, I knew we were in danger.

The mate sang out: "Stern, all!"

We dropped our oars and gave one shove astern, just as the whale made a side sweep with his flukes, cutting off the head of the boat and hurling the mate into the sea twenty feet away. The third boat picked him up and started for the ship. Our boat sank, but by laying the oars across the gunwales and standing on them, we could keep our heads above the surface of the water. The second mate was still fast to the whale, and as we stood in the water up to our necks, the monster came rushing towards us making a horrible noise. I thought he was going to run us down, and sang out at the top of my voice: "Come back with that boat!" but the officers did not heed my call. He came within twenty feet of us then turned aside. We were in the water about half an hour, when the boat returned for us, and were so cold and numb that we had to be hauled on board.

The second mate tried to kill the whale, but our accident had evidently unnerved him. His men said he would sing out: "Stern, all!" before he was near enough to use the lance effectively everytime they attempted to approach. It was now about sundown and the captain signalled to cut line and come aboard.

On examination it was found that our mate had been struck on the left leg, and the bone crushed from above the knee down to the foot. Mortification set in in the course of a few days, and the doctor amputated it above the knee, but the operation did not arrest the process of decomposition. It extended to his body and he died. The day following his death we buried him in the mariner's grave, with no tombstone but the stars. He was a nice man, well liked by all. His name was Payne and his home and family were somewhere on Long Island.

That day's whaling cost one man his life. The property losses included two stoven boats, four harpoons, five lances and about one hundred and fifty fathoms of line, or about

$125.00. Whereas, if they had exercised due caution, I think all this might have been avoided, and the whale captured. He would have been a valuable prize worth several thousand dollars, for all agreed in estimating that he would have yielded four hundred barrels of oil at least

After the death of Mr. Payne, the second, third and fourth mates were promoted a grade each, and a man from the fore castle was made harpooner or fourth officer.

We now shaped our course south southeast, our next objective point being St. Paul's Island, in thirty nine south latitude, Indian Ocean. We reached it the last of February, laid off and on two days, and went ashore with our boats.

Four Frenchmen and four black slaves constituted the population of the island. They were engaged in catching fish, (salmon, I think) and salting and drying them to sell. The blacks were branded on the face. I do not know to what tribe or nationality they belonged.

The island is surrounded with seaweed called kelp, and the water is alive with the fish I have mentioned. We went to shore with the boats and caught eight barrels of them. These were the fattest fish I have ever seen. We salted them down.

The island is an extinct volcano, or, to speak more accurately, the rim of the crater. The sea fills the crater and the tide ebbs and flows through a break in the wall on one side. Through this opening small boats can enter the crater at flood tide. At the right of the entrance there are hot, boiling springs. The exposed portion of the rim rises several hundred feet above the water. Steps have been cut in the lava or rock, by which you may climb to the top. A large flat rock rests on the summit, and on it is inscribed the names of many ships and the date of their visit to the island. The island is circular in form, and, I should judge not more than two miles across.

On the evening of the second day, after we were all on board and preparing to set sail, the captain, full of fish and rum, and the new mate had a lively time. I was aloft loosening top-gallant sails, and could look down and see the fun. It looked at one time as though there would be bloodshed. I heard the captain bawl out: "I will let you know that I command that gun!" referring to an old rusty cannon on the forecastle deck. The other officers succeeded in quieting the row before serious consequences resulted.

There was another trouble brewing between the captain and Dr. Winslow, and shortly after leaving St. Paul's Island it culminated in an open rupture. It commenced about Mary, the doctor's servant girl. She was a freckle-faced, witty Irish girl, and developed a fondness for sitting on the quarter deck moonlight evenings, to listen to the officers relate stories of their travels and adventures. Sometimes she would linger until quite late. The doctor, or his wife would reprimand her, telling her that she ought to come below earlier. A man of the captain's windy characteristics could not forbear to interfere. He objected to what he termed the doctor's "cruelty" to Mary, as an unwarrantable restriction upon her liberty. To the captain's officious intervention the doctor replied that he thought he knew his own business. Harsh words ensued and the controversy waxed hotter and hotter, until the captain went so far as to draw a revolver on the doctor. The latter then withdrew, saying, "I will settle this with you some other time." They did not speak together again during the voyage, but the captain annoyed the doctor by ordering a man, our Neptune subject, to stand sentry before his door, walk to and fro and at short intervals drop the butt of his musket on the deck to keep the doctor and his family awake. The girl was seldom on deck evenings after the row.

On the twentieth of March, we had left the Indian Ocean

behind us, and Van Dieman's land was visible off our starboard beam. The wind was blowing fresh, the barometer indicated a heavy storm and we began to prepare for it. We shortened sail, battened down our hatches and lashed everything movable. As the wind increased we continued to shorten until only our storm sails were set. This was the worst storm I ever encountered, and for nearly five days we fled before it with the wind on our starboard quarter. But the Margaret Scott was a good sea boat, and rode triumphant the mountain waves that seemed, each moment, to threaten inevitable destruction

Standing on the main hatch, forward of the mainmast, when the stern would settle into the trough of the sea, we could look over the mizzen top and see a great wall of water that appeared as though it must surely engulf the ship. But the stern would rise as we ploughed ahead and the great wave divided and went roaring past her sides.

I watched the old stars closely to see if they showed signs of fear, but could detect no difference in their looks or actions. They appeared to be as jovial as in calm weather, and I took their apparant unconcern to mean that we were all right.

During the first three days of the storm, the captain did not appear on deck, then he came up, took a look around and said: "The old ship has weathered it remarkably well!"

It was the second day of the blow, as I recollect it, that we shipped a sea that stove two of our small boats and the cook's galley. The galley filled instantly with water, and the old negro cook popped out head first blowing like a porpoise and followed by chunks of beef, pork and whatever else his quarters contained that would float. He came up stroking the water from his chin whiskers, saying: "Blow! debbil, blow! you can't carry away dese fellahs!"

This mishap entailed the only losses we sustained from the storm.

Fine weather followed the gale. The carpenter repaired the whaleboats and cook's galley. On the 15th of April we encountered a school of young sperm whale, killed five of them, and they yielded one hundred and twenty barrels of oil.

The following day we sighted one of the Windward islands, of the Society group, called Toboai. It has no harbor. We ran in near shore, landed with the boats and purchased some hogs, potatoes, yams and fruit.

I was between decks cleaning blubber, when I heard a strange jabbering on deck. Looking up I saw human beings, who wore nothing in the shape of clothing save a small fringed mat about the loins. I thought they must be wild men, their appearance was so singular.

We sailed at dark, and about noon the next day sighted the island of Tahiti. We were favored by the prevailing southeast trade wind, and before night the low, flat lands of the coast were visible from deck.

We hauled up the cables, gave them a turn around the windlass, run them out through the hauser holes and bent them onto the anchors. Unlashed the anchors from the rail and hung them to the catheads, ready to lower. Thus prepared we laid off and on until morning, then ran in and anchored under guidance of a pilot. It was now seven months, two weeks and four days since we left New Bedford, including time given to whaling.

As we approached the island the breeze came off shore laden with the fragrance of tropical fruits and flowers, and the attractions of a beautiful, tropical landscape greeted our vision. All was new and strange to me and I was anxious to go ashore.

The bay shore is semi-circular or crescent shaped, and a coral reef forms the outer harbor, seaward. It is not a land-locked port, but affords good anchorage and is roomy enough to accommodate quite a fleet of vessels. Ships from all parts of the world stop here for fresh water and provisions, or for traffic.

CHAPTER III.

FAREWELL TO WHALING.

The doctor gets even with the captain—Rum and bilge water—Deserting the ship—Exciting experiences—Meet shipmates—Visit the Windward Islands —Incidents of the trip—Return to Pata—French vs. natives—Battle o Point Venus—Missionary shot—Tahita—Characters and customs of the ra tives—Aboard the Shepherdess.

Tahiti was then, and is yet a French possession.

On shore, the captain continued to abuse Dr. Winslow whenever they chanced to meet. The doctor had studied medicine in Paris, and was familiar with the French language. He made complaint to the French authorities of the island, and had the captain arrested and put into the calaboose. He was in three days, and was escorted by a French officer while attending to his business in town. The American Consul arranged for him to stay on board of the ship nights.

While he was in the calaboose, one of our sailors was put in for drunkenness. He accosted the old captain, saying: "How do you like this fare, old hoss?—I'm as good a man as you are, here!" The sailor paid $5.00 fine, and was released. I think the doctor was even with the captain.

Two of the officers and some of the sailors joined in making complaint to the consul, that the captain's drunkenness incapacitated him for managing the ship. The consul had the balance of his rum emptied into the ship's hold and pumped out with the bilge water.

When we had been in port about a week the men began to desert the ship. The French were at war with the natives, which made it comparatively easy for them to escape, as the natives in town sided with the French, and did not dare to go back into the woods to hunt sailors for reward or bounty, as they had done formerly.

I was determined to go too, but thought it best to wait until the ship was nearly ready for sea, before taking "French liberty," as the sailor calls running away. They had shipped some new hands and did not allow the men to go ashore. The old cooper had deserted, and we were waiting for one that had been sick in the hospital. The old negro steward came to me and said: "Bill, let's run away!" I told him the old ship was all right. He belonged to the cabin and I dared not trust him.

During one of my excursions on shore I discovered a break in the rear foundation wall of a Kauaka church. The aperture was small but I could squeeze through, and the floor of the building was high enough above the ground to allow me to sit up. I decided that here would be a safe and available hiding place, and laid my plans accordingly. I managed to stock my contemplated retreat with a small quantity of sea bread, and patiently awaited a favorable opportunity to take my departure.

The opportune moment came at last, when the ship was nearly ready to sail. The officers were in the cabin taking dinner. A native was fishing along side, and I gave him some sea crackers to put me ashore. The first man I met was the captain, under escort of a French officer, engaged in shipping men to fill vacancies caused by desertion. He said to me: "Where are you going, and what are you doing on shore?" I had to make some excuse, and told him I was after a man who owed me a couple of dollars. "Be right back and go aboard of the ship!" he commanded. Aye, ayo, sir!" I replied. I hurried on until I reached the outskirts of the village and laid low until dark. As soon as I thought it safe, I went to a French restaurant, bought a couple of wine bottles, filled them with water and conveyed them to my hiding place under the church. I ventured a second trip, bought two loaves of baker's bread and put them in my frock, a loaf on each side. As I came out of the restaurant, the boat steerer came along with two men carrying the new cooper's chest from the hospital to the boat landing. The harpooner was a nephew of the captain's. He said to me: "You intend to desert come along with me and go on board of the ship." He is considered a petty officer, so I walked along, but meant to fight rather then go aboard. As they went down to the landing, I wheeled and ran in another direction, with Charley after me. It was getting dark. Right ahead was the bridge that spans the spring brook which is about ten rods wide at this point and filled out with bogs and mud. My pursuer was gaining on me, and I turned aside and leaped into the brook. It was a long ways around and he gave up the chase. I wollowed across, sometimes sinking to my knees in the mud, and came out in an old Frenchman's yard on the other side. The dog came after me and the proprietor swore, heard him say something like sacra mon dieu. This demonstration only helped me along, as I knew that I was not wanted there. I reached my harbor of refuge under the church without further mishap, laid down to rest, and think over the exciting experiences of the day. It was Saturday night. I soon discovered that my troubles were not ended. Something was crawling in the sand, and fearing it might be snakes I dared not go to sleep. When morning came I saw that the disturbers of my rest were a colony of harmless little brown lizards that disappeared in their holes as soon as it was light. As poor company is better than none, I rather enjoyed their presence than otherwise, after the first night. Services were held in the church the following day but my presence was not discovered nor suspected so far as I know.

My retreat was safe, but otherwise barren of attractions. By the end of the third day I was decidedly weary of my enforced seclusion; and, as my supply of water was exhausted and provisions getting short, I determined to make a break for the woods and endeavor to reach the table land above the town. I started about daylight in the morning and traveled through the ticket until I reached the highlands. Fearing the natives would see me, I climbed into an orange tree and sat there all day. I ate of the fruit but found that orange juice is not very strengthening. I was getting weak and hungry. At dark I started again. It was a bright moonlight night and traveled over the highlands until I was tired, then laid down until daylight. In the morning I walked on towards the mountains until I reached the forks of the spring brook alluded to heretofore. I found that it divided and a smaller branch made its way to the coast by a widely diverging route. Each traversed a separate valley, and these embraced the highlands over which I had journeyed, the same converging to a point near the fountain head, a large spring near the base of the mountain, proper. It was about two hundred feet down to the floor of either valley. The larger one varied in width from twenty to eighty rods, and as far as the eye could reach groves of lemon and orange in rich profusion studded the level bottom land. At frequent intervals stately cocoanut palms towered above their lesser associates. I had never seen the like, a grand and gorgeous landscape, once seen, never to be forgotten

Here and there in the larger valley a native dwelling could be seen among the trees. The smaller valley lacked the lemon and orange groves and was not inhabited. The bluff was precipitous, but I clamored down, hanging unto the bushes, until I reached the lower level. When I had rested, I attempted to climb a cocoanut tree, but made poor headway, as I had not learned the native knack. I persevered until I could reach a nut, laid hold of it with one hand, exerted all the strength and weight I could bring to bear, and at the same time maintain my hold upon the trunk; but without avail. I grew weak, and had to slide to the ground and take a rest. I tried it again with the same result. At the third ascent, I secured two nuts. By placing my hand over the upper end and giving them a quick jerk, I found that they snapped off easily. I subsisted on cocoanuts and I a mnas four days. I could live, but could not lay up anything. I kept house and washed my clothes and at the end of that time started for the coast, following a path that eventually crossed the Broom road and brought me out at a place called Townoa, five miles from Pata, the harbor. I met two of my shipmates, and found that the carpenter who came out with us as a passenger was keeping house here. We took dinner with him. I learned that our ship had sailed two days before.

Here I found a topsail schooner that wanted men and got a berth aboard of her. She belonged to the natives, sailed under French colors, and was manned by an English captain and crew. She was bound for the Windward Islands after a cargo of potatoes and yams. The French suspicioned that she was smuggling arms and provisions, landing them up the coast at Point Venus for the hostile natives and kept pretty close watch of her movements. We sailed, and the fourth day came to the island where we received our cargo. There was no anchorage, the ship laid off and on, and we brought the freight off in the boats.

One day the weather was rough and we took refuge under the lee of the island until the wind abated. Next day as we were coasting back to where we were receiving cargo, the French cutter came around a point of land ahead and ran down towards us before the wind. Our captain ordered: "Hoist the colors, quick!" We run them up but they wound around the signal halyards, as if ashamed to float. When in hailing distance, the commander of the cutter ordered our captain to bring his clearance papers on board. Our captain replied: "The sea is so heavy it will swamp our boat." The cutter ran out a thirty two pounder, and our captain ordered us to lower away the boat without further parley, and we went aboard the cutter with our clearance papers.

The old Corsican was walking the quarter deck, and our captain went aft, hat in hand, and submitted his papers to him. When he had inspected them he said: "I have a mind to take you back to Tahiti, but will permit you to continue your voyage, and will report you to the Commodore." The Frenchman's gun did not make us feel friendly towards them, and we decided, unanimously, that this should be our last voyage under the French flag. We brought the schooner back to Townoa, turned her over to the owners and all hands quit. I think the cargo was for the natives, and some dark night was put ashore at some point up the coast.

From Townoa I returned to Pata.

The French governor of the island resided at Pata, martial law prevailed and sentinels were stationed throughout the town. A cannon was fired every morning at sunrise, and again at 9 o'clock in the evening, when everybody had to be under cover, or on board a ship. If they caught you out later they would put you in the calaboose and you had five dollars fine to pay in the morning.

Beside the cutter that overhauled us on our voyage to the Windward Islands, the French had a steamer cruising about, and the frigate Euraine, with the Commodore aboard, lying in the harbor.

An English cutter was anchored in the bay, the frigate Collingwood cruised outside the harbor, and Salamander laid at Amro, a small island in sight of Tahiti. All were evidently watching the progress of affairs.

Pomae, queen of Society Islands, did not like the French, would not stay on shore, and was entertained on board the English cutter.

One day the French transport, Bourbonais, came into port with army stores and four hundred soldiers on board. She engaged an English pilot. When coming through the entrance the wind was light, she did not mind her helm, the tide set her onto a rock, stove a hole in her bottom and she partly filled with water. They lightened her of part of her cargo and the steamer towed her off, but she sank before reaching her dock. They thought the pilot did it purposely through malice, and he was arrested and put in irons. There was enmity between the French and English officers. The French tore the flag from the English consulate, trailed it in the dust, and perpetrated other insults.

The English commander ran in and conferred with the French Commodore, on board the Euraine. The latter agreed not to molest the natives further until they could hear from their respective countries. But the next day the French sent three hundred soldiers up the coast to Point Venus, opened fire on the natives and burned their dwellings.

The English missionary located there politely asked the officer in command not to burn his house, but it was in flames a few minutes later; and the missionary was killed purposely, or by a stray bullet. The English cutter sent a boat and brought him to Pata, where he was buried.

The Salamander steamed over from Amro, ran into the

harbor and challenged the French Commodore to come outside the reef and settle matters, but the Frenchman declined the invitation. Many expected that these troubles would lead to a war between the two nations. The French lost seventy men that day at Point Venus. The natives were sheltered by the thickets and cocoanut trees, and reported only three killed.

I went up in company with some other boys, and we were watching the battle from the beach, but when we saw the old missionary fall we concluded that we had better return to Pata.

Tahiti lies in about 15° south latitude and 150° west longitude. It is one of the prettiest islands in the south Pacific and is called the "garden of the seas." It is about one hundred miles in length by seventy-five in breath. Its highest mountain rises above the clouds, its summit divided into four peaks. From the side of this mountain bursts the great spring, the fountain head of the brook heretofore described.

When you enter the harbor of Pata, one of the most beautiful landscapes on the globe greets your view. The beach is skirted with a low growth of cocoanut trees, interspersed with lemon and orange. Flowers everywhere, their rich perfumes permeating the atmosphere. The native dwellings nestling under the trees adds life and picturesqueness to the scene. All along the beach groups of boys and girls are seen sporting in social glee, some sitting, others promenading, all happy, seemingly, as nature itself. Canoes shoving off for a fish in the bay, others returning laden with finny prizes. They are a light-hearted, happy race of people and their merry laughter is heard on every hand. All in all it is a scene never to be forgotten.

When compared with savage races generally, these people present many striking and pleasing contrasts in national characteristics and social customs and conditions. They are a very mild tempered and affectionate race, living in the utmost harmony among themselves. Worshippers of idols and subjects of darkness and superstition for unknown ages, they possess in a high degree of the amiable qualities generally supposed to pertain to more enlightened races. These extraordinary features were noted by the first white man who visited these islands.

The island is very healthy. There is no wet or marshy land. The climate is perfect, temperature varies but little from 80° Far. the year round, perpetual summer without excessive heat. The low or flat lands run back to the foot hills or tablelands, in some places ten to twenty miles in width, while at some points the highlands come down nearly to the sea. The valleys along the streams are great orchards of lemon, orange and other fruits. These vast natural plantations loaded with their rich yellow fruits are splendid to see.

Point Venus, heretofore mentioned, is a spur of the mountains that approach very near to the coast. Here astronomers have met from time to time for the purpose of observing eclipses and to study the stars. The Broom road runs nearly around the island, built by deserting sailors and convicts. The group was under English control a good many years but they had traded Tahiti to France for some other possession. The natives were dissatisfied and several battles were fought before they were finally subdued and compelled to submit to the sway of France.

They were converted to Christianity, had contributed money and joined with missionaries in the work of converting other groups. They are a very interesting people.

[Perhaps some may think that the foregoing account of the captain's arrest and confinement in the calaboose is somewhat exagerated, as he is understood to be, and in fact is a monarch at sea; subject, of course, to the marine laws. But on shore he is a private citizen, amenable to the local laws. Furthermore, because of war between the French and natives, Tahiti was under martial law at this time, and Dr. Winslow was commissioned by our government as hospital physician at Mauee.]

I stayed on the group about two months, then shipped on the brig Shepherdess, owned in Sydney and commanded by Captain Schoots. I met the captain and hailed him for a birth. He said he wanted a man. "What is your wages?" I asked. "Two pound ten," replied the Scotchman. "All right," said I, but did not know how much it meant in Yankee money. He told me where the brig was anchored and I went aboard. There I found the mate a big Scotchman, six sailors, and the captain's wife, a very pleasant and social lady.

CHAPTER IV.

TRAFFIC WITH THE NATIVES.

The brig's equipment and business methods—Island of Rarotonga—We entertain visitors—The captain and the cannon—The Samoan group—How we lost our anchors—The Fijis a treacherous people—Girl offered for a musket—Remarkable differences in character—The Chain Islands—Taken sick and left on the Friendly Islands.

The Shepherdess was suitably fitted out for the business of trafficking with the natives; and in the pursuit of trade visited all the South Pacific groups, receiving cocoanut oil, turtle shell, dried bananas and such other native products as were salable in the Sidney market, in exchange for goods of the white man's make. A successful voyage returned good profit to the owners.

When we came to an island that had a harbor we would run in an anchor, but as most of them did not possess this advantage, we would heave to as near shore as practicable. The fancy goods and notions were then brought and displayed on tables in the cabin, so as to catch the eyes of our prospective Kanaka customers. On each quarter deck was a small cannon on pivots, and these were fired to notify the natives that we were ready for business. Soon a flotilla of canoes could be seen approaching the brig, some laden with cocoanut oil, others with turtle shell, fine mats, a pig, chickens, fruits, vegetables, etc. When the trading began it reminded one of the confusion of tongues at the Tower of Babel.

Our stock included muskets, axes, hatchets, looking-glasses, beads, cloth, and most of such trinkets as are usually kept in a Yankee notion store. The captain's wife was a good saleswoman; like many of her sex, a great linguist and slight of hand. At some islands they had left barrels the previous voyage, to be filled with oil, and at some places we could find four or five of these barrels filled and ready for us. We paid a fair price for oil and such other commodities as sold well at Sidney. The oil, turtle shell, and mats were the most valuable. We paid a mere trifle for the fruit.

We visited a beautiful little island called Rarotonga. It has a bay where vessels of light draft can enter. A missionary and his wife were the only white inhabitants. It was a cozy place to live. Our captain and wife invited the missionary and wife, and the king and his family to come on board and take dinner with us. We sent our boat after the guests, and fired salutes while they were coming from shore. They had an enjoyable time and were well pleased with their visit. We had prepared to fire a farewell salute while they were returning to land, but when we applied the match the guns refused to go, and we did not succeed in firing them until the boat had reached shore. This irritated the captain so much that, when we had succeeded, he continued to fire them until near midnight. He said he would throw them overboard if they ever went back on him again. We stayed at this island ten days, then sailed for the Samoan group.

We touched first at Apia and did a little trading; passed on and dropped anchor at a larger island called Tutuila. Here we received several barrels of oil and some fine mats. The captain had dealt with them before and they had prepared the oil for him. They were very nice natives to deal with. It is a nice island, and there were some white residents beside the missionaries. The whites had built a small schooner of about twenty-four tons burden, called the Petrel, and she had taken some of our trade. She did not run to Sidney, but traded with groups near by and sold to other traders.

When ready to depart we essayed to raise our anchor, found it was fast under the coral reef and had to wait until morning, when we tried it with the windlass but could not fetch it. Then we made sail and attempted to trip the anchor. After several trials the cable parted and we had to sail without an anchor, as the brig had previously lost the other in the same way.

We sailed for the Fiji group, and at the expiration of three days came to a large island called Lakimbau. The natives came off in canoes bringing fowls and a little oil. Our captain would not go ashore as they were a treacherour people, and we might have trouble with them. Some were cannibals and might want to make a feast of us. We bought seventy-five pounds of turtle shell, several gallons of oil and some fine mats. They offered to trade us a girl for a musket. At night we drove them ashore, made up our minds that we would not trust ourselves in their company any longer, and sailed away. Subsequently, I became better acquainted with them, as they are near to, and frequently visit the Friendly Islands.

We traded at some groups where the natives seemed to be lower down in the scale of humanity, but not so treacherous, of mild disposition, and very simple hearted, appearing more like children. When we had made a trade with them they wanted more. For amusement the sailors would sell one of them a ring, bolted to the deck, and of course possible to separate therefrom. He would pull at it a long time, then sit down and cover it with his tapper thinking it might become loose, and when he thought we were not looking would try it again. Sometimes they would cry because they could not succeed.

The natives of the Chain Islands, a group situated a few degrees north of the equator, are expert swimmers and noted divers. A French ship sank in the harbor of Tahiti and they hired some of these natives to dive and fasten to the anchors and sails. The Chain Islands are not as productive as some of the other groups.

The natives of some groups are surly, have an ugly disposition and it is difficult to trade with them.

It is strange there should be such marked differences in the characteristics and conditions of the natives on the different groups so near to each other.

On some of the islands, not yet visited by missionaries, converts from other groups had taught them to forsake their sins and love Otua. But some are slow of comprehension and made slow progress. Time has wrought a change, no doubt. Some may think they are all Christianized but they are not half civilized. Heathen nature needs watching by the missionary, you will find.

Captain Cook gives us some idea of certain groups in his account of his voyage around the world; but it would be difficult to name two where the native characteristics and disposition are identical. Compare any two that you please and you will find one superior to the other intellectually, and in the exhibition of mechanical genius. These will respond to the influences of civilization and improve their condition as they become enlightened; while others seem dazed at the superiority of the white man's ships, equipment and knowledge. It would seem that they at once regard it as impossible for them to attain to the higher possibilities of life, the prospect discourages them, they abandon ambition, become lazy and apathetic, and are sunk below their native status in the scale of humanity by contact with civilization. If I remember rightly, Captain Cook notes this in the journal of his last voyage that they were not as industrious and thrifty as when he first visited them.

On some islands they punish criminals by making them beat gnato or native cloth. On other groups no attention is paid to the offender.

I think there are some small islands that will never be settled by foreigners.

Generally speaking, it may be a question whether these islanders have been benefitted by contact with civilization, or not. The missionary comes and tells them they must be good and love one another. The words and actions of the next white man that comes among them are not in keeping with the teachings of the missionary. The native is quick to note the inconsistency, and I have often thought that the influence of the evil doers more than counterbalances the opposing force. If the white man's religion, is all the missionary claims it to be, it is incomprehensible to these simple children of the isles that all white men are not Christians. To them it is a great stumbling block, and retards the success of missionary work.

When we had cruised from group to group for several months and the brig was about ready to sail for New Zealand, we touched at the Friendly Islands, situated in 18 and 19 south latitude and 170 west longitude. Tonga is the largest of this group, and is said to be eighty to ninety miles in length. Near it are a number of smaller islands, or motus. The next in size is Vavau, distant about two degrees from Tonga. Midway between them are eleven smaller islands, called the Habias. I can name the most of them: Tongua, Harfeva, Oua, Namuka, Lafouka, Kau, Tofua. Have forgotten the names of the remaining five. These were not inhabited. The soil is of volcanic origin and very productive. Nearly everything required by the natives grows spontaneously. Yams, sweet potatoes and tarrow are cultivated. The tarrow looks like white turnip. It is dried and pounded into flour, then made into pudding, and is a very wholesome food. Bread fruit, bananas, lemons, limes, oranges, cocoanut, pineapples, lashe, etc. grow without cultivation. Very little labor is necessary to afford them a living, as nature has provided nearly everything they need.

It was my lot to be taken sick about this time, and they left me on one of the small islands called Harfeva, and it transpired that I remained on the group about three years.

It was in the month of August that I was put ashore and the brig expected to return about the first of January, following. The captain left six barrels to be filled with cocoanut oil during his absence. I had my choice to go with the vessel or stay on the island, and decided to remain. The natives told the captain they would take care of me, and he agreed to recompense them when he came again. But the Shepherdess did not return, and I heard afterward that she was sold for debt. I was unable to walk and had to be carried ashore.

CHAPTER V.

LIFE AMONG THE NATIVES.

The old lady doctor—Primitive barbering—Lafa Lafa—An exciting experience—An object lesson—Learning the language—Go to Tonga—A native festival—Mr. Thomas, and his unregenerate charge—The bark Jane Eliza—The darkey steward again—News of the whaleship—Earthquakes—Go to Vavau—Interpreting—Choosing a tamai—Joseph Arnold—Work of the missions—Native characteristics, etc.

I was now alone with the islanders, sick, helpless and entirely at their mercy. I could not understand a word of their language, and they were equally ignorant of English; but they were kind to me. An old lady doctor took me in charge, and the first thing she did was to shave the hair all off my head with a mussle shell, called *Neichfingota*. I would not care to patronize a barber indefinitely who used a razor of that description, but it did its work well, if it did pull. They think it a good thing to do, and practice it in treating their own sick. She dosed me with roots and herbs, but my appetite was poor. The old chief, my host, would take up a chicken leg with his fingers and hand it to me saying: "*Kaikai hanga koi tagata tonganei,*" meaning, "eat like our people." I would shake my head. The old doctor woman brought me some sugar cane, took off the crust, and I could eat, it tasted good. She next gave me cocoanuts that had sprouted, the milk of the nut being about the consistency of a mellow apple, and I could relish them. With these she kept me well supplied.

They named me *Nanea*. I do not know what the name is derived from.

The chief's family consisted of himself and wife, a boy

about fourteen, a girl of sixteen or seventeen, and a female relative a year or so older, as near as I could judge their ages.

I shall never forget a little incident that happened the third day of my stay on the island. The old chief and his wife were away, visiting, I suppose. The young folks amused themselves a long time playing a game called *lafa lafa*. A fine mat is laid down with two opposite sides turned under, forming a trough. Each player is provided with a hard, smooth, flat nut about the size of a silver dollar. Two or four can play and twenty is the game. The first player slides a nut across the mat to as near the opposite edge as possible and not fall off. The second endeavors to knock it off and leave the nut he throws on the mat; and so on in turn to the end of the game.

When they had tired of the game, the boy, because of a longing for excitement, a little natural vindictiveness, or both, bethought himself to have some fun at my expense. The native weapons of war were stowed overhead. He pulled down a war club and walked up to me. I was sitting on a mat, unable to rise and stand upon my feet, to say nothing of walking, running, or defending myself in any way. He brandished the club about my head until I thought he meant to kill me. The girls cried: "*Tongaua! tongaua!*", meaning "stop! stop!" He suspended hostilities with the club, took down a spear and amused himself by thrusting it past my head, so close that I feared he would hit me; but I could not help myself and had to take the insult.

About four o'clock the old chief returned, and I could see by the looks of the girls that they were telling him what had happened. He would cast a look at me, and while they were talking the boy went out. The old man followed him, but soon returned armed with a heavy whip and marching the youngster in front of him up to within a few paces of me, he went at him, and I have never seen anyone get such a mauling before or since. I motioned for him to desist, but he seemed to lay it on the harder and finished the job to his own satisfaction. I felt that I should be protected after that. I played with the boy frequently after I got able to go out, but he never alluded to the affair, and would do anything for me.

My experiences of the first few weeks present an object lesson, forcibly illustrating the fact that it is very easy to be mistaken. I might as well have been a mute, as I could not understand, or make myself understood in words. Sometimes a party of a dozen or more would gather at the chief's house, some of them savage looking men. I would sit for hours, listening and wondering what they could be talking about. They might be plotting to kill me for all I knew, and I watched the changing expressions of each face to see if I could detect treachery. Imagine yourself in my position and suppose that a burly savage of forbidding countenance and in ugly mood, (as he appears to you) should approach and say: "*Jut afa kiackoi.*" Another of milder aspect and friendlier bearing comes and says: "*Tamata kiackoi.*" You would doubtless be terrified by the first, but conclude that in the second comer you had found a sympathizer and friend. When, in fact, the former has addressed to you the beautiful national salutation, meaning: "My love to you." While the words of the latter mean: "I will kill you. I had some queer thoughts and unpleasant feelings as I watched them, and passed some sleepless nights before I learned to talk with them.

My old doctor woman attended to me faithfully, I wanted for nothing that she could get for me, and at the end of six weeks I could walk in good shape. From this time on I mingled with the natives and went about the island as

I pleased. Learning their language was the hardest work, which took me about ten months.

When I had been on Harfeva about eleven months, two large canoes from Vavau stopped at the island, on their way to Tonga to attend a native festival. The party consisted of about fifty persons including the Tui, or king. I embraced the opportunity to go where I could see a missionary. We left Harfeva about 3 o'clock in the morning and arrived at the island of Tonga that same evening, a little after dark. I found a missionary by the name of Thomas. He had been located there about four years. He seemed very glad to see me, and invited me to stay with him while the natives were holding their festival. I stopped at his house about four weeks

Less than half of the natives of Tonga had been converted at this time. Mr. Thomas generally had a number of the unconverted, usually boys and girls, staying with him to receive religious instruction. When I was there he had two boys and three girls with him, all converts except one girl. The latter was a keen black-eyed girl, who was always playing tricks on the rest of us. We used to repeat a verse and repeat the Lord's prayer in concert every night.

One day the unregenerate female began to torment me in various ways. I told her that I would tell the missionary, if she did not stop; but she kept it up until I picked up an old coffee mill that lay out in the back yard and threw it at her. She threw things at me until I got tired of it and threw a yam. It struck her, knocked her over, broke, and a piece struck against the missionary's door and made quite a racket. The next morning after breakfast and prayers had been disposed of, the missionary asked us what the trouble was. I did not feel in the best of spirits that morning, and told him I thought I had better go before I killed some of these wild subjects. Told him further that I thought the quickest time I could make would be plenty slow enough. He tried to smooth the matter over, but I went and stayed with the natives until the festival ended.

Mr. Thomas wanted me to help him talk to the natives and make converts. I told him that I lacked the patience; thought I could do more good, and better missionary work by ordering my actions to conform to his teachings, that I always gave them the best advice I could whenever I had an opportunity.

The bark Jane Eliza, of Sidney, came into port. She had sprung a leak and been condemned by the officers. One day I was sitting near the beach and noticed a negro walking back and forth along the shore. I thought it strange he did not speak to me. Finally I went towards him and he began to show his ivories. I said to him: "You black son of Africa, what are you doing here?" It was the old darkey steward of the whale ship. He said he knew that I was afraid to trust him when he proposed that we desert together. He swam ashore the next night after I left. "How came you here?" he asked. I gave him a brief account of my adventures since we departed on board the whaler. He gave me some information as to what befell the Margaret Scott after we left her. About two weeks out out from Tahiti the captain died and they gave his body to the sharks. The "old hoss" had finished his last voyage The officers brought the ship back to Tahiti and refused further charge of her. A United States cutter conveyed her to Sydney, Australia, where she was put in charge of some one to finish the voyage, or take her home.

One afternoon about four o'clock, I was under an orange tree with some other boys. Suddenly we heard a rumbling sound resembling distant thunder, and the earth began to vibrate. The leaves on the trees would turn up first on one edge and then on the other. The disturbance lasted only a few seconds and the rumbling sound passed on beyond our hearing. This was my second and last earthquake. My first experience was on Harfeva. One night while I was preparing for bed. I felt things rattle and heard the natives crying: "*Koi mofuike!*" That was a word I had not learned up to that time and I said: "*Kui hai?*—What is it?" I found it signified that the island was moving. I thought that is what we call an earthquake. It was only a slight shock and there was no noise. They are not desirable visitations and give a person queer sensations.

After the festival was over we sailed in the canoes for Vavau, the second island of the group in point of size. We stopped over night at a small island and reached our destination the second day.

An English missionary and family by the name of Turner were located at Vavau. Two vessels, the Tryton and John Williams brought them supplies from Sidney twice a year.

I had the best possible opportunity to learn the natives' characteristics, usages and customs, as I was with them all the time, and when ships came to the island I did the interpreting for them. When you go among them to live they want you to choose some chief, or other person as your *tamai*, or father, and you are regarded and treated as a member of his family. Their object is to have you help them in trading with the ships that visit them for that purpose. As I could talk both English and Kanaka, I did most of the trading for them, and the ship's captain would pay me something as well as the other parties.

There was another white man on the island beside the missionary and myself. He was about fifty-five years of age, an old sailor, and a native of the state of Maine. His name was Joseph Arnold. He had been struck by a whale and his shoulder and hip broken. He had lived with the

Kanakas longer than I, but could not speak the language. He was a blacksmith by trade.

The natives are a happy race of people and seldom have any contention among themselves. They are governed by a tui, or king, and chiefs called aga and hoaga. They have but few laws and these are made by consent of the majority duly assembled. The code is simple and they have no use for lawyers. They have a large building, called, *farle fonu*, or house of law, where they meet once a year, where such changes as may be agreed upon, if any, are made. The king, the chiefs and all who desire may come and take an interest in hearing and enacting the tabus.

Idolatry had been abolished throughout the group, excepting the large island of Tonga, where only about one third of the natives had been converted at the time of which I write. In their heathen state they worship the sun, or *Laa* as the source of all light, and the moon and other objects as lesser deities. They have been slow to change their superstitions regarding marriage and burial of the dead; but the missionaries have wrought a wonderful change in them since they have been among them. They would often ask me if we were all Christians in Amalika. I had to admit that such was not the case. They thought it strange, as we had the Bible and were enlightened. I explained in this way: Some will never be Christians under any circumstances, because they are controlled or influenced by a *laumalie oku kovi*, (a bad spirit) while others were influenced by *laumalie naoni oni*, (the holy spirit.)

The schools were taught by the missionaries and their wives, and were yet in their infancy. They had a small hand printing press and had published leaves and pamphlets, and translations of portions of the Bible, (of the New Testament, principally) into the native tongue. Old and young could be seen going to school with these leaves in their hands, all evidently anxious to learn. They had printed some small hymn books, also, and many of the pupils could read and sing very well, considering that they had been under instruction only a short time. The missionaries drilled them nearly every day and exhibited great patience in teaching them. They held morning, afternoon and evening meetings, and singing was a regular feature every session.

I learned the alphabet of the young man who run the printing press, and can read some. Nearly all of the letters have the broad sound.—i is e and e is a. Example: Tagata, a as in car. There are not as many letters as in the English alphabet.

They are fond of company, very social and great talkers. They have gatherings, festivals and amusements nearly every week, and are very friendly and kind to each other.

Comparing the pagans on the island of Tonga with their converted neighbors, I could detect very little difference in their mode of living. They traded and mingled together in social intercourse without contention. The missionary and converted portion had tried to frighten them into Christianity by threats of war, but to no purpose. They were ready to fight rather than give up their way of worship, and the attempt to coerce them was abandoned.

Their worst enemies were the Fiji islanders, with whom they fought several battles. The Fijians were the aggressors, coming to attack the Friendly islanders in large canoes. They always went away satisfied that they were whipped.

The Fijians are a quarrelsome people. They appear to be a different race from the natives of any other group in the South Pacific. They are different in feature, darker of complection and are fierce, warlike, treacherous and restless in the extreme. I have talked with them about their meanness, but they did not care to converse on that subject.

They are a large, well formed, athletic people, able to endure any amount of hardship. The Fiji group comprises about eighty islands. The climate is fine and all tropical fruits grow to perfection.

I understand that they have since been converted to Christianity, the Friendly islanders assisting the missionaries materially in the work.

CHAPTER VI.

LIFE AMONG THE NATIVES.—*Continued.*

The native dress—Manufactures; cloth, mats, etc.,—Cooking—Bread fruit—The cocoanut tree and fruit—Marriage ceremony—The feitoka or native cemetery—Turtle hunting—Rambles in the interior—The tabued grave—The missionary's goat—The vaka or native canoe.

The natives are very clean and tidy, considering the way in which they have to live. The dress consists of a vala made from the bark of a tree called tutu. This tree is about four inches in circumference and about eight feet in height. The bark being very tough and strong is stripped off in one piece. It is then soaked in salt water, and the brown or outside bark which is very thin is scraped off with a knife or shell. The strip is then laid over a smooth timber and beaten with an instrument called *ika*, i. e. a square stick about a foot long, with two smooth faces and two grooved lengthwise. Beating with the grooved sides spreads the bark and with the smooth sides reduces it to even thickness. The finished strips are about one foot in width, and when they have prepared a sufficient quantity they paste them together, three layers thick, and the finished product is colored in stripes and checks. The coloring matter is obtained from a certain nut. A fine mat with a braided fringe, called a *chichi* is worn over the vala. The headdress completes the native costume, and is made by plaiting small fibers of cocoanut husk, interwoven with a small perfumed bud called *kakala*.

As the temperature is always warm they never suffer from cold, or *momoko*, as they call it.

Sometimes they buy cotton cloth of the traders. They had not learned the use or value of money, or *paanga*, but bartered their commodities for hatchets, flint lock muskets, lookingglasses, beads, blue or brown denims, etc. It cost but very little in shipping to get supplied with all the fresh provisions needed. At that time you could buy a pig that would weigh from 100 to 150 pounds for *ofa ua*, that is two reaches of cloth with the arms outstretched. The natives paid a good price for everything they got.

The islanders had a rude and novel way of cooking. In the first place they built a *beto*, or cook-house. Then in the center of the earth floor they dug a hole about four feet in width by two in depth and paved the bottom with small cobble stones. When the pig (which is always roasted whole), and the vegetables are ready, a fire is built in the oven and kept burning until the stones are properly heated, when the coals are raked out and some small limbs are laid over the stones, on which the pig is laid. A few small stones are heated, wrapped in dry banana leaves and placed inside the pig. They have a large leaf called *lepa*, about the size of a large cabbage leaf, that is tough. Four or five of these are firmly pinned together with cocoanut leaf stalks, and the oven is covered four or five inches thick with these pads of *lepa*. Over this is placed a layer o soil about two inches thick. After about an hour they scrape off the layer of soil, remove the *lepa* covering, and the pig and contents are found baked as nicely and evenly as anything you ever saw. They bake once a week, but never eat warm food, or use warm drinks. They think it injures the health and is bad for the teeth. I think they are about right, as I never saw one of them with decayed teeth.

The cooked meat is cut into small pieces, wrapped in dry banana leaves and hung up. The atmosphere is so pure that it seldom spoils. Neighbor divides with neighbor, and they accommodate each other without stint.

The bread-fruit tree grows luxuriently, is an abundant and perpetual bearer in most of the south sea islands, and furnishes wholesome sustenance without cultivation. The natives are very liberal and supply ships with fresh provisions for little or nothing. Uninhabited islands are stocked with hogs and fowls, free to all the world in cases of shipwreck. There is plenty of cocoanuts, fruits, etc., for them to feed on, and left to themselves they thrive and multiply.

The bread-fruit tree attains a height of from ten to twenty feet. The leaf is much the size and shape of a maple leaf. The fruit is borne on small branches of the large limbs, is a little oblong in shape, is about as large as an average sized cabbage head when fully grown, and of a greenish color. When cut a milky substance oozes out, and it is not good to eat raw. It is very white after it is baked, but has a centre core that is not good to eat. There are other ways of preparing it. One method is to pound, knead, roll and cut it into small pieces. These are placed in a dish, sugar-cane juice and cocoanut milk is added and the whole cooked over a slow fire until it thickens and resembles sweetened cream. The natives called it *feikekai*. It is an extra dish with them an most anyone would relish it. In whatever manner prepared, the bread-fruit is a healthful and very nutritious food. The tree has economical value beside the fruit. The limbs are used for rafters in building their houses. They are tied together with *kafa*, and are of sufficient strength to sustain the light thatch of cane or cocoanut leaves with which they are covered. The bread-fruit is a staple article with them.

The cocoanut tree is called *niu* by the natives, and its fruit is of great value to them. It grows luxuriently without care or culture. When ripe, the nuts fall to the ground and lie a year or more until the rainy season comes on and moistens the husk and the soil. You have noticed the three circular spots, or scars near the large end of a cocoanut. In one of these the shell is thin enough to be easily pierced with a pin, and from it the sprout starts. The kernel, or meat consists largely of albumen and furnishes nourishment for the young plant; and the milk furnishes moisture. The tree begins to bear when eight to ten years old, and continues to bear for many years. Full grown trees are about two feet in diameter, and from sixty to one hundred feet high. The nuts grow on a stem very much like grapes, and may be seen in all stages of development on the same stem, from ripe nuts at the base to blossoms at the apex. The fruit stems grow out from the base of the leaves. From this tree they constructed their houses complete without using a nail. The frame work is tied together in nice shape with *kafa*, or sinuet. Kafa is made from the husk of the nut and is very strong, and is used for many other purposes, such as fish lines and nets, boat building and larger ropes. Their roofs are thatched with the leaves, their floors are carpeted with mats braided of same, called *takapau*, and mats form the doors and walls. They make combs of the split ends of leaf stalks.

The sap is used as a beverage. To obtain it, a blossom stem is cut off above the nuts, and a dish made of a shell called a *hohonie* is hung beneath to catch the flow. From one to four quarts of sap are obtained from each stem. It tastes like sweet cider, and by distilling it the natives get a sort of liquor that is very intoxicating.

To get the oil, the nuts are broken, then scraped over an iron with teeth filed into it and nailed to a piece of timber. The meat or oil substance falls into a trough, and when it is full it is set in the sun and covered with a thin mat, and the oil runs out after it stands a while. The oil is sold to traders and yields quite a revenue. They use the oil for anointing the body, and when deliciously perfumed with sandalwood, for oiling the hair. They make very serviceable baskets of the leaves by splitting the mid-rib and bending the halves together to form the rim, then plaiting the leaflets. The milk of young cocoanuts is much used for drinking and cooking. The shells are scraped, polished and ornamented for dishes. They fatten their hogs on the meat and use the shells for fuel. Most of their cordage is made from the fiber of the husk. The cocoanut palm may be said to be the mainstay of the Kanaka.

VAKAMAU, or Marriage Ceremony.

A marriage is a gala occasion, celebrated by feasting and general rejoicing. In anticipation of the event, the friends and relatives of each contracting party roasts pigs and bread-fruit, and prepare the most elaborate spread of viands the country affords. In the fore part of the day set for the ceremony, the groom's party exchange what they have prepared for that contributed by the bride's friends, and they eat, and drink *kava*, and have a social time until about four o'clock in the afternoon, when they all assemble together. The contracting parties meet, shake hands and sit together, and the feasting continues until all are satisfied. The couple then comes forward and stand before the *aga*, or chief. The chief's wife brings wreathes of perfumed buds, and places one upon the head and another around the waist of each. The *aga* then gives them some good advice, and pronounces them man and wife. A dance by moonlight usually closes the festivities. They dance in a circle, or waltz. They have reeds of different sizes and lengths that they play with considerable skill, making very good music.

Since the missionaries have been among them, they marry them over again according to church formula. As man and wife they live together in harmony, and divorces and family quarrels are unheard of. In many respects we might pattern after them to our advantage. Their moral character is good (speaking of the Friendly islanders), and are a thrifty and tidy people, keeping their *abas*, or yards, clean and in good order. They take pride in raising yams, bananas and other fruits.

A cemetery, or *feitoka* as they call it, is enclosed by a wall of cocoanut logs four feet high, and the entire space filled in level with the top of the wall. When one of their people dies they wrap him in native cloth, and bury with him some of the implements he has used in life. If he was a warrior, a war club, or spear is laid beside him. After the grave is filled with earth they bring baskets of small, white pebbles and sea shells and lay them on the grave. The baskets are made of cocoanut leaves, as heretofore described, and after they have been once used for this purpose, it is *tabu*, or against the law to use them for anything else, and they throw them into a hole and never touch them again. It was their heathen custom to howl and cry for three days, lamenting for the departed, but they gave this up when they embraced Christianity.

During certain months of the year the turtles come up on the beach to lay their eggs, choosing, generally, the outlying, uninhabited islands. The natives go over in canoes and hunt them, armed with spears, or sticks. When one of them sights a turtle he makes a rush at him, and the turtle makes for the water, all the time throwing sand back with his claws, as a defense. But they turn him over on his back and he is captured. The shell is cut off dried and prepared for sale to the traders. At that time it was worth four dollars a pound in Sydney. It is manufactured into combs and other articles.

When I first came to the island of Vavau, the natives were all strangers to me, of course. But I went freely when I pleased. I would start off on a tramp, following their paths or *halas*, and penetrate into the interior. It was a beautiful country. At many places the limbs of the trees interlocked over the path. At intervals of two or three miles I would come to villages, or settlements of half a dozen houses, perhaps, delightfully situated amid the groves of orange, banana, and bread fruit. The children playing in the shade would be the first to notice my approach, and run to the house crying "*papalangi*," meaning foreigner. I would go to the house and say: "*Jut ofa kia koa*," that is "my love to you," their usual way of accosting each other. The reply would be: "*Takanofa*," that is "come in and sit down,"—wondering that I could speak their language. After talking awhile they would express themselves as very glad that I came to see them, and I often remained four or five days. They would ask me all about *Amalika*. When I would tell them of the cold (*momoko*) so severe that rain (*fefeka*) gets hard, they would shrug their shoulders and say: "*Takoi manavaha*," meaning, that beats all. It was very hard to explain about railroads and many other things so that they could understand. Sometimes I would be gone two weeks at a time, wandering from one settlement to another, and found them always a hospitable people, eager to listen and learn all they could about other countries.

I was walking with a native one day, some distance from any settlement, and we came to a certain thicket. He pointed to it and said: "There is a place that is *tabu* for us to go." I asked him what he meant by saying it was *tabu*, and he related this story: Some years previous there were two men living on the island, one a Cape Verde Portugese and the other a Spaniard. They both fell in love with the same native girl. At a party one evening, the girl was eating a piece of sugar cane. The Spaniard asked her to give him some of it, and she refused. The Portugese said: "I think she will divide with me," and said to her: "*Makonga toa?*" and she broke it and gave him a part. The Spaniard was offended and jealous, and that night he went to the house where the Portugese staid and killed him. "An eye for an eye and a tooth for a tooth," is the native law They pursued the murderer, and on the third day they caught him in this thicket, clubbed him to death and buried him where he fell. He had a bad spirit (*laumalie*) and no native would go near his grave.

As we traveled through the woods we came across droves of pigs all sizes, running wild, fowls of domestic breed that had been in the thicket so long that they would run, fly and skulk under the bushes at our approach.

The Friendly Islands are very well timbered, but very little use is made of it except for fuel and canoe building. There was at one time quite a trade in sandal wood, but it had been mostly cut off, or died out.

Some of the islands are well supplied with good fresh water springs; others have no fresh water at all except what they catch in cisterns, but the milk of young cocoanuts is the principal beverage of the natives.

Sugar cane and sea island cotton grows on most of the groups.

The Friendly islanders are a healthy, well formed, athletic people, of a light brown color. Some of them are as white as the English. They are expert swimmers, and have killed sharks with knives. They told me of two young women who swam from Tonga to Oua, a distance of eight miles, on one occasion when they were at war with the Fijians.

One time when the missionary vessel, Tryton, came in

with supplies, she brought with the rest a two wheeled cart, to use in transporting the goods from the landing to the warehouse. As the missionary was going away that day to preach on a small island near by, he requested me to procure some native boys and oversee the work of hauling and stowing the goods left by the vessel. I engaged the services of about a dozen boys, and they did the hauling by means of ropes attached to the cart. They would sing as they trudged along, making a fearful noise, in full chorus. As we approached the warehouse in the back yard, we passed a narrow lane, fenced with reeds about eight feet high, that led up to the back door of the mission house. This door consisted of two sections, like a mill door. To the left as you entered the door, was the dining room, and the table was spread for dinner. The back and front window of the dining room were in line with the place where I stood, and I could see the interior plainly. The missionary had a large goat that furnished the milk for tea. As we swung into view, with the vocal band in full play, I noticed the goat in the lawn, and that the upper half of the door was open. I saw at once that the animal was frightened by the noise, and I tried to stop the boys, but they did not hear me. The goat selected the door as the only means of escape, and leaped over the closed half. The girls screamed, the goat rushed into the dining room, sprang upon the table and swept cloth, dishes and all to the floor with an infernal clatter, and the next bound went through the window carrying glass, sash and all into the front yard. The boys left me in a hurry and hid, Mrs. Turner came out and lectured me severely. She used no profane language, but looked very much like it, said she would never have thought it of an Englishman. But she soon saw that I was not to blame, as I could not manage a piratical crew of boys. The old man came home next morning. He met me with a smile and said: "You had bad luck, but I cannot blame any one, as accidents will happen." I asked his forgiveness.

In building the *vaka*, or native canoe, they first erect a boat-house in which the canoe is built and kept until ready to launch. The material is accumulated and the craft planned. Then, as we would say, they make a bee, and on the day set as many as forty may be seen engaged in the work. Some making *kafa*, or sinnet with which the planks are fastened together. Not a nail or piece of iron of any description enters into the construction of the vessel. Some are hewing planks for the sides. The planks are dressed with a groove on both edges. The grooves lap one into another as the planks are built together, pierced with holes and the joint laced firmly with *kafa*. When the timber is not of sufficient length, they splice the ends so that they cannot pull apart. All the joints and seams are calked, or gummed with a material of their own make. Some of these canoes are seventy-five feet long, fourteen foot beam, with four to six feet depth of hold. When the large canoe is finished they build a smaller one, and the two are placed about ten feet apart and fastened together by cross beams decked over. In sailing the craft, the small canoe is always kept to windward. It takes about two years to build one of this magnitude, as they only work on it at intervals, and are provided for the use of the king or missionary. The method of sailing the *vaka* is very ingenious. The short mast, working on a pivot, can be slacked over to either end of the canoe. When they get under way the yard is hauled up to the head of the mast, then inclined at such an angle that the mast, the yard and the deck form a triangle; the halyards acting as stays. When they want to go about the mast is slacked over to the reverse, the tack and sheet change places and the stem becomes the stern. They can steer from either end, as bow and stern are alike. The sails are woven of rushes or bark. With a fair breeze, the craft is capable of making fifteen knots an hour.

CHAPTER VII.

LIFE AMONG THE NATIVES.—*Concluded.*

Joe Arnold, pilot, and the missionary's cast off beaver hat—Piloting and interpreting—Joe's blacksmithing outfit—Our business flourishes—Chief Nafau, my tamai (father)—Sad fate of a young whaleman—Flogging a brutal punishment—A better way—Capt. Benj. Price of Boston—Of the natives; their history, manners, customs, etc.—Capt. Bligh's estimate—Old Joe and Captain Clark—Natives of different groups compared.

On this group of thirteen islands there were only four white men, the two missionaries, Joseph Arnold and myself. I have mentioned old Joe heretofore. He was a happy dispositioned, queer old genius. As he was a blacksmith by trade, it was his ambition to get a bellows and a few tools, so that he could do work for the Kanakas. He sat thinking for some time one day, and finally said to me: "I have thought out a plan, and if it works I believe it will help us. We have heretofore assisted ships to enter the harbor, free of charge. Hereafter we must act as pilots and get paid for our services. I am going up to old man Turner's and see if he has a plug hat I can borrow, or buy; that will make us look dignified as pilots should. Perhaps I can get material for a bellows, and a few tools. I think it will pay." So away he went to see the old missionary. In about half an hour he returned with the hat. It had seen its best days, but we repaired it by wiping it, pressing out the short kinks and applying a little cocoanut oil to lay the nap and restore the polish. About three weeks later the natives sighted a ship in the offing, standing in towards the island. We engaged two natives with their canoe to take us out to the inlet of the bay, about three miles. We put on our best rigging, Joe wearing the hat and sporting a cane; we made quite a respectable appearance. When we met the ship, she backed her main yard and hove to. We went on board and asked if they wanted a pilot. The captain asked our price. Joe told him one dollar a foot for the water she drew, seventeen feet, and take it in trade,—clothing, etc. Money was not legal tender at that time. The captain said: "All right; take charge of the sailing of the ship." There was only one place in the bay where there was good anchorage; that was in eight fathoms of water. The rest of the bay was from twenty to forty fathoms deep, and we might have run the jibboon into the bushes anywhere without grounding the ship. There was absolutely nothing in the way of coming to the anchorage, but the old pilot would have the men changing the course, or shifting sail to avoid an imaginary shoal or rock. And I would be tellling the men in the hearing of the officers, that Joe was an accomplished pilot, and knew every foot of ground in the bay. We came to an anchor all right. Joe bought material for a bellows; canvass, pitch, tar, nails and an old gun barrel to serve as a nozzle or pipe to carry wind to the forge; some tools,— tongs, hammer, files and a small vice. The balance of our pilot's fee, and five dollars additional that I got for interpreting while they were securing supplies, we took in clothing and other articles. After our return home, we would have a good time cuffing the old beaver up to a peak, then we would slick it up again for the good it had done and hang it up to await the arrival of another ship.

We next had the Kanakas bring us a log about eight feet long, borrowed a pit saw from the missionary and made lumber for the bellows. When the frame was made, we covered it with the canvass, applied pitch and tar, and when all complete we had quite a respectable looking and serviceable bellows. It was not nearly as air tight as many I have seen, but it made wind enough to make the wood and charcoal sparkle, and answered our turn very well.

One day two natives brought an old musket that would not stand cocked, and wanted to know what Joe would charge to repair it. The smith said: "Bring me four good hogs, one hundred cocoanuts and twenty yams." They asked when the gun would be ready. Joe told them about one week. All Joe did was to file the notch in the dog, polish the old firelock up a little and it was all right. It took him about half an hour. They brought the stipulated fee, and the articles thus obtained we sold to trading vessels. Joe said to me: "I told you it would pay."

The natives bathe regularly every morning, considering the practice essential to the preservation of health. They know nothing of their orgin or geneology. I often questioned them on this subject, but could gain very little information, as they had never invented a method of keeping records. Their traditions are vague and indefinite, dating back to the time of some favorite ruler, Fenau, for instance, who was a good king. They had no method of computing time, and could not tell their ages. Since the missionaries came among them, they have taught them the scheme of the calendar and something of our method of dividing and computing time by days, weeks, months and years.

In their towns or settlements, each dwelling stands in an *aba* (yard) about one half acre in extent, enclosed by a neat, serviceable fence. To build the fence, posts are set in the ground at regular intervals, to which small poles are securely lashed with *kafa*. A reed, called *kahu*, is cut in lengths of about eight feet, set upright close together, like pickets, and lashed to the poles, completing the structure. Each dwelling comprises four separate *falas* (houses.) They cook in one, dine in the second, sleep in the third, and the fourth is the general living or sitting room. Sometimes accommodations are provided for others beside the family. The lots were square, of uniform size, and separated by *halas* (streets) about twelve feet wide, which was sufficient, as they had no teams or vehicles of any kind.

Old Nafau, my *tamai* (father), was the chief that ranked next to the king. His wife, my *fae* (mother), was named Alieka. He was a very good man. He had a house built for me. It took four men about four days to do the job.

A whaleship from New London, Conn., stopped at the island for fresh provisions. I made the acquaintance of one of the crew, a young man about twenty-five years of age, from Hartford, Conn. His manners and conversation indicated the gentleman of refinement and education. One day he told me his story. He was the son of wealthy and respected parents, and a college graduate. If I remember rightly, it was disappointment in a love affair that caused him to go to New London and ship aboard the whaler, contrary to the wishes of his parents and friends. Once out at sea, he began to reflect and regretted the rash step he had taken, when it was too late. He had signed the ship's articles for the voyage, and must abide by the contract. He tried to persuade the captain to let him go at the first harbor they entered, but the captain told him he had no authority to discharge good men.

I was attracted to the young man from the first; his sad story and evident distress completely won my sympathy, and when he asked me to assist him in getting away from the ship, I told him I would do the best I could. He expressed his gratitude, and said he would reward me for my kindness, if we should ever meet in our own country. He said the whale ship had become so disgusting to him that life aboard of her was unbearable. I told him I was sorry for him and would do all in my power to secrete him until the ship went away.

I have described the large canoes and mentioned the fact that they are kept stowed in a large building, erected for the purpose, when not in use. As the natives seldom use these large sea going craft, I selected one of them as the most available retreat for my protege. Every night I carried him eatables, and cocoanuts to drink. The officers looked for him, but apparently gave up the search and put to sea. After the ship had been gone three days, the young man concluded there was no danger that she would return, and came out of hiding. The missionary vessel was expected soon, and he thought he might get passage in her to Sydney, where he might stand a chance to get a ship home. I found him to be as represented, a gentleman in every respect. About sunrise on the morning of the fourth day, we were talking together near the landing, not thinking of danger, when the chief officer and four men came upon us. They were so near when we discovered their presence that retreat was impossible. He gave himself up, but told the officer he would never do any more work on the whale ship. The ship had laid off and on, standing out to sea during the day and returning at night. I had heard of this trick before, and had warned the young man that they might play it on him, but he thought the ship had gone. He felt bad, but had to go. I saw one of his shipmates two years later, in Honolulu, and learned his sad fate. After they got him aboard of the ship, he refused to work and they seized him up to the rigging and whipped him terribly. Again he refused to work and they stripped him the second time and flogged him until the blood ran down his back. He finally went to work and sometime afterwards was one of a boat's crew that went after a right whale. They fastened to the whale and the monster struck the boat with his flukes, threw it into the air and killed two men. . My friend was hurt, or killed by the blow, as he did not rise to the surface and was never seen again. When the sailor told me of his death, I felt as though I had lost an intimate friend.

I consider flogging one of the most disgraceful and brutish punishments that man can inflict upon his fellow man, and it is well that it has been abolished. No officer ever practiced it without gaining the ill-will of his men, that sometimes culminated in mutiny.

I think there is a better way than to flog men. An instance that occurred on board the ship I came home in will serve to illustrate. One of the crew was a Scotch boy. He was at the wheel, the second mate spoke to him, thought the boy's answer did not show due respect to the dignity of a superior, and had him seized up to the rigging. While the officers were at dinner the men cut him down and had him in the forecastle taking his dinner. The officer came to the companion way and called for the boy to come up on deck. We told him he would come when he had eaten his dinner. When the boy went aft, the captain met him and talked to him as a father would to a son. It did the boy more good than a dozen floggings. That was Captain Benjamin Price, of Boston; that was his way, and his men all respected him. He was then a white-haired old man of seventy-two years, had made eighteen East India voyages, and served under Commodore Perry, on Lake Erie, in the war of 1812 This was his last sea voyage.

How were these islands inhabited? How and from whence did they come? nearly three thousand miles from the mainland, Australia being the nearest. They have no knowledge of navigation, or vessels suitable for so long a voyage. There are several groups, Society, Samoan, Friendly, Fiji, New Hebrides and others, and it is a remarkable fact that the Fiji islanders are a different race of people than are found on the other groups, darker complectioned, different in feature and disposition. They have been harder to civilize or Christianize. The Fijis are surrounded by the other groups. If the original inhabitants had been driven from some distant shore, lost at sea and finally landed on one of the groups, from whence they gradually spread from island to island, naturally they would be all of one race.

The natives never venture far from their own islands. The southeast trade winds blow from nearly the same direction the year round, and with the sun and stars serves to guide them from one island to another.

When I was with them in 1842, a few were yet living who remembered Capt. Cook, and showed me presents he gave them when he stopped there on his voyage around the world. They had no recollection or tradition of ships coming to their shores before his time, and it must have been many years, if ever.

They have no idea of their origin, or from whence they came. They worship their *otua*, or God, believe in *lau malie* or spirit, believe in and practice circumcision and worship idols. I have seen some of their idols and talked with them about their worship, but could gain no definite ideas from them. They are a very singular people. They do not increase rapidly or their islands would be overrun, and their *feitokas* (cemeteries) are not large. The islands would support a dense population, as half the area might be converted into the richest of gardens, and the other half be sufficient for the natural fruit groves.

They are very careful sailors. When going from one island to another they start early so as to sight land before dark. If the winds are light they use their paddles, also. In that latitude the nights are short. I have made voyages of several hundred miles with them, and had no fear that they would not make the passage safely. These seas are seldom swept by heavy storms, and with sails taken in the canoes will stand pretty rough weather, but would not prove seaworthy for long voyages; and I do not think the natives originally came to the islands in similar crafts, as emigrants from some foreign shore.

One day, as Joe and I sat together swapping tales of adventure, the natives reported another ship in sight, headed for the island. We gathered up our outfit, gave the old beaver a good brushing, boarded our canoe and went out and met the ship. This was the third ship we brought into the harbor. Joe mounted to the deck with great dignity, and as soon as the captain saw him he called out: "Hello! Joe Arnold, is that you?" Joe replied: "Helio, Capt. Clark, I never expected to see you again this side of our happy home!" "Well, Joe," said the captain, "you appear to be all right." Joe said: "Do you want a pilot?—that is my business at present." "Can you take us in?" "If I can't, this old beaver can." 'All right, the men will obey your orders." We brought the ship to anchor and had supper with the captain. During our conversation, he said to Joe: "I am homeward bound, and if you will go home with me, you will fare as good as I, and need not do a hands turn." Joe had made three whaling voyages with him. Joe replied: "Captain Clark, you see that rise of ground?" (pointing shoreward) "that is our *feitoka* or cemetery. I shall lay my bones there,— if you would give me half of the city of Boston, I would not go home with you." "Well," said the captain, "I think you have a pleasant place to live here and a fine climate; I will not urge you, but would like your company home." "Thank you, Captain, I am satified here with the Kanakas." Captain Clark appeared to be a fine man. He paid us twelve dollars pilotage. I assisted him in purchasing supplies, for which he paid me liberally.

The British ship, Bounty, was sent to these islands by the English government for the purpose of collecting bread fruit plants for the West Indies. She remained six months, and the following extract from the report of her commander, Captain Bligh, is a just tribute to the natives:

"They were a mild tempered, social and affectionate race, living in the utmost harmony among themselves, and their whole lives being one unvaried round of cheerful contentment, luxurious ease, and healthful exercise and amusement. The women are handsome, mild and cheerful in their manners and conversation, possessed of great sensibility, and have sufficient delicacy to make them admired and beloved."

They were very kind to me, and wished me to remain with them, but I was young and wished to see other parts of the globe. I have never found a better or more healthful climate than these islands, but the thought of being so far away from civilzation made me lonely at times; but I have found that it makes but little difference where a person is, if he is contented with his lot.

In going about among the different groups, I learned something of human nature, and had an opportunity to note the changes wrought by civilization. There is a marked difference in customs and usages regarding the female sex. On some groups they are treated as menials and slaves, compelled to cultivate the gardens, get the fuel for cooking and do all the drudgery. On other groups the men treat them kindly and as equals. They are only required to attend to their household affairs and make the native cloth. Those who treat their women with kindness and respect are a better class of people, always,—less treacherous, and easier to civilize and Christianize. The Fijians or Mulgrave natives treat their women like brutes, and sometimes kill them because they do not make good warriors. Christianity has bettered their condition, but it has cost the lives of some good men to instill a sense of right and justice into their savage and preverse natures.

CHAPTER VIII.

MY TRIP TO THE NORTH.

Bidding adieu to the Friendly islanders—Old Joe's lecture—Reflection, "The Mariner's Grave—Arrive at Petropaulovski—Furs and salmon—A trip into the country—A clam bake—The Kamtchatkan dog—Start for the Hawaiian Islands—We encounter a gale—Arrive at Honolulu—My seaman's permit—The Hawaiian group—Kamchameha III—Tars and Poe—The great volcanoes—Capt. Cook's monument—Meet an old friend—The boarding house and the milk bottles—A day on horseback—The "Blonde" dance house—Sailor characteristics—Pastimes at sea—The gonic.

When I had been on the islands nearly three years, a ship came that wanted a man. She was bound for Kamtchatka and Behring's Sea. The owners had agents at Petropaulovski procuring seal skins and other furs. She came around the cape of Good Hope, touching at the islands of Java and Borneo, in the East Indies. I shipped for the trip, to terminate at the Sandwich Islands. I bade adieu to my old father, Nafau, the chief who adopted me. They did not want me to go.

I next informed old Joe of my intention to leave the islands. He looked at me, and this is the lecture he gave me: "You little fool! What is the matter with you? What ails you? You will never find another place like this on the globe. I have sailed every sea on the face of the earth, and you will never find a place where you can live as easy as you can here. I think you are getting crazy!" I said to him: "You have seen the world, and are getting old. I am young, have not seen much of the world, and do not feel like spending my younger days here."

When we were out of the harbor and had secured our anchor on the bows and cleared the deck, I had time to reflect, and to think over my experience with the natives. I looked back at the island, recalled my trials, my "ups and downs", the care the natives had for me, and felt grateful to them. They had taken care of me without expecting to be rewarded for their trouble, and I told them in grateful and kindly remembrance.

I found the captain and crew a very pleasant lot of men. The bark was a good sailer, and everything went on smoothly. We ran past the Mulgrave Islands, near which the whaleship Essex was sunk by a sperm whale, and some of the crew were killed by the natives. We sailed in May, and nothing of importance occurred during our passage to the north.

After we arrived in the sea of Kamtchatka, we spoke a ship. One of her crew had recently died and they had buried him on a lonely island, with a rough box for a coffin. They thought it the right thing to do, as they were near the island when he died, and the crew volunteered to take him ashore. One of his shipmates had composed the following verses in memory of the event, and they gave us a copy:

THE MARINER'S GRAVE.

I remember the night,—it was stormy and wet,
    And dismally dashed the dark wave,
As the rain and the sleet, cold and heavily beat
    On the mariner's new made grave.

I remember; it was down in a lonesome dell,
    And near to a gloomy cave;
Where the wild winds wail 'round the wanderer pale,
    That we dug the mariner's grave.

I remember how slow the bearers trod,—
  And sad was the look they gave,—
As they rested their load near its last abode,
  And gazed on the mariner's grave.

I remember a tear as it slowly slid
  Down the cheek of his messmates brave;
As it fell on the lid it soon was hid,
  For closed was the mariner's grave.

Now o'er his cold bier the brier is trod,—
  The wild flowers mournfully wave,
And the willow weeps, while the moonbeam sleeps
  On the mariner's silent grave.

It was in the month of August that we sailed along the coast, and it was very warm in the valleys; but the mountains in plain view, were covered with ice and snow. The sharp contrast, always striking, is marvelous to him who sees the like for the first time. The seasons are of too short duration to raise vegetables or crops of any kind successfully. We ran up the harbor about eight miles and dropped anchor at Petropaulovski, a Russian penal colony. It has a dock for the use of ships taking or discharging freight.

On a high piece of ground to the left of the landing were about twenty dismounted brass cannons, which must have lain there for years as they were nearly covered with soil. When they were brought it was intended to build a fort, but the work had been suspended because of lack of funds. The first building to the right of the quay was a church with a chime of bells. I think it would compare with Noah's ark in architectural design. The other buildings and shops were much after the same pattern, and most of them built of logs. Our ship's agent resided here with his family, and bought furs and salmon, for her New York owners. The country abounds in seal and other fur bearing animals. It is a great place for salmon, and immense quantities are salted and dried for export. They feed their dogs salmon and dried bear's meat. The winter dress is made of fur, and one garment is so constructed as to encase the entire person, including head and feet. A peculiar kind of dog which never barks, is the most valuable domestic animal. All the timber used for fuel and building purposes is hauled on sleds, by these dogs, during the winter season. They are also used to carry the mails over the mountains into Russian Siberia. They will travel all day without stopping to feed, and make better time than the reindeer. The latter must have dinner, and will break through the crust where the dog will not. Carpenters, blacksmiths and other artisans were located here. The woodworkers draw the plane towards them instead of pushing it as we do. It looks awkward, but their work looks well when finished.

We were given liberty one day, and took a trip into the country. We saw a few small farms, but the products were confined to turnips or potatoes and a few other vegetables, and some oats and hay. It is a wonderful country for wild berries, and they grow in great variety and abundance.

At the time there was a French, a Prussian and a Russian war vessel in the harbor, besides our bark. We had a pleasant time with the boys, considering the number of languages we were obliged to murder. We could all drink wine, or *atka*, they called it, and it made us all talk about the same tongue and feel happy for two days.

The days were very warm until about sunset, when we would be attacked by a swarm of the largest and most voracious mosquitoes I ever saw. The sailors called them the Russian eagle. About midnight they would crawl into the bushes.

One day our agent and family, the Russian nobility, and officers of the several ships, with four boat's crews, armed with spades, shovels, picks, baskets and tubs, went out about six miles into the bay, clamming. Provisions and other necessaries had been provided for a good time. We reached the clam grounds at ebb tide, and found a large surface of sand bare of water. The sand was full of small holes. We would thrust the spades down beside these holes, the water would spurt up bringing the clams to view, and we gathered several baskets and tubs full. We carried them ashore, dug holes in the sand, built fires, covered the clams with hot sand and they were soon ready to eat. When the nobility had dined, the sailors finished the rest. In the meantime the others were having a good time by themselves, and finally began playing "one old cat," as the boys call it, with spades, picks and shovels for bats, and baskets and tubs for balls. To hear the confusion of tongues, one would think that Babel was about completed. There were some bloody noses when the fun was over. At flood tide we loaded the fragments into the boats and pulled for the harbor, arriving about sunset.

During the summer months, they chain their dogs along side a small stream of water, and feed them, except the "leaders," which are allowed to run at large. They are a short eared, bushy tailed dog, and when the bells begin to chime they all set up a howl, and it is impossible to hear anything else while it lasts. It is a hard looking place to live.

We set sail one afternoon, and when we got inside it began to blow a gale. We were in a large bay, and had a hard time beating off shore, but when we were clear of the land we headed down the coast for the Hawaiian Islands. One day as we were running near the coast we heard a noise like cannonading, and looking in shore through the ship's glass, we could see whale's flukes rising and falling, and every stroke on the water sounded like the report of a heavy cannon. They were sulphur bottom species sporting in the bay. After the gale we had fine weather, made a good run, and came to anchor in the harbor of Honolulu, on the 15th day of October.

Here the voyage ended for me. In order to remain on shore, a sailor must take the oath of allegiance, or obtain a "seaman's permit," at a cost of $2.00, good for sixty days, and must be renewed when the time expires, or take the oath of allegiance. I obtained a permit, of which the following is a copy:

SEAMAN'S PERMIT.

{ ROYAL }
{ STAMP }

Permission is given to Lawrence Fosdick on board the Ar. B'k Acasta St., now lying in the harbor of Honolulu, Hawaiian Islands, to remain on the island of Oahu, for sixty days, he being discharged from the obligations of his shipping articles by his captain.

Port of Honolulu, Hawaiian Islands.

Oct. 30th, 1846. P. PENBALLOW,
per ARTHUR PRITCHWOOD.

The islands are in about 19-24 north of the equator. Some of them are very nice islands Ten islands are comprised in the group. Oahu is the capital island. It is not the largest, but has a passable harbor, protected by a reef breakwater, seaward. Honolulu is the capital. In 1846 Kamehameha III was king, but the islands were practically governed by the English. The missionaries were Americans. The soil is of volcanic origin and produces most of the fruits common to the tropics.

There are stretches of rich level lands along the coast, bearing large cocoanut groves, sugar cane and sea island cotton. No use was made of the cotton and cane at that time. The *taro* root was extensively cultivated, and formed the staple article of the food of the natives, especially of the poorer class. It grows in low, wet lands and resembles the turnip. It is dried, pounded into flour and made into a sort of porridge called *poe*. It is a very wholesome and nutritious food. Knives and forks had not come into fashion in Honolulu at this time, and the natives ate with their fingers. It was said of the *poe* that the upper classes made it thick and used one finger; the next class lower made it somewhat thinner and used two fingers, the poor made it still thinner and used four fingers; the very poor made it very thin and used the whole hand. Hence, there was one finger, two finger, four finger and whole hand *poe*. Whether this was true or not I do not know. Those I saw eating used one or two fingers.

The natives were a kind and simple race, but they have learned the evil habits of foreigners, such as drunkenness, thieving and prostitution. It has been the hardest task of the missionaries to counteract the evil introduced by depraved foreigners, but they have done good work.

I remember seeing King Kamehameha on his way to church one Sunday morning. He had on a plug hat, checkered swallow tailed coat, white pants and vest, and sported a cane, but was barefooted. He looked comical.

The group of islands contains about six thousand square miles. The climate is fine but the natives are degenerating and dying out. Mauna Loa, in Hawaii, is the largest active volcano on the globe, and the extinct crater of Mauna Haleakala, on Maui, is by far the largest known. I visited the latter, and was down the coast as far as Diamond Rock and the Weiititi plains.

King Kamehameha was expert with the spear and war club, and appeared to be fond of sport. He would allow four men to throw spears at him at a time, and he would ward off the spears and catch them in his hand. He appeared to be respected and well liked by his subjects.

The natives are good swimmers, and will stay in the breakers an hour at a time with their surf boards. They are a singular people. They killed Captain Cook in Kalakua Bay. A cocoanut stump coated with pitch and tar, is the monument that marks the spot where the tragedy occurred. Whenever a ship stops here the sailors add a new coat of pitch and tar to preserve it. The natives deeply regret the crime.

One day, as I was walking up the street in Honolulu, I met a lady with a basket on her arm. I noticed that she was looking at me rather sharp, and as she came up to me she said: "I believe I know you, I think you are one of the sailors who came from America, around the Cape of Good Hope to the island of Tahiti." I was surprised, but recognized her at once as Mary, the former servant of Dr. Winslow. She was glad to see me, and I asked her what she was doing in Honolulu. She told me she had been married more than two years, to a good, kind husband, and had two children. I congratulated her on her good fortune, and said to her: "You are worthy of a good man, and if you can talk as well as you could on the "spouter," you can entertain him." She replied: "Yes, I used to have as much lip as a right whale, as the men would say. I try to make it pleasant for my husband. I should be glad to have you call and see us." I thanked her for the invitation. I did not see her again, but it seemed like meeting an old shipmate.

There was but one first class hotel in Honolulu at that time. The other stopping places were one story board buildings, where seamen boarded. The sleeping apartments were small board houses, with nothing for beds but mats spread over straw. The house where we boarded was provided with a long table that would seat thirty persons. Half a dozen mechanics boarded at the same place. I presume that milk pitchers were not in fashion, as the milk was brought to the table in small black bottles, and these were invariably placed at the head of the table where the carpenters sat, and by the time they found their way to old Jack tar's end of the table they were empty. One morning we held a consultation; the partiality shown to the carpenters was unanimously condemned, we fixed upon a plan that we thought would insure a fair distribution of milk in the future, and proceeded to carry it out. We went in to breakfast, and as soon as we were seated the old salt at the foot of the table sang out: "Scull Black Betty down this way!" The moment the order was given the bottles went sailing the whole length of the table, followed by potatoes, etc. The landlord, trying to quell the riot, said we should have fair play and made us all sorts of good promises.

After breakfast we concluded to take a cruise down the coast. Fifteen of us went to the stables and hired horses to ride, as there were few vehicles at that time. The price was two dollars each, in advance, for the use of horse, saddle, bridle and whip. These horses never trot but go at a gallop if urged off a walk. When we were out of town, we stopped and chose a captain and other officers to command the fleet, then set sail down the coast. It was a fine flat country for miles back from the coast, largely occupied by groves of cocoanut, orange and lemon, and patches of *taro* and pineapple. Native dwellings were scattered through the groves. We stopped occasionally and talked with a Kanaka who could speak a few words of English After cruising a few hours the order was given to about ship and steer for home. We had ridden a short distance on our return, when one of our crew sang out: "Sail, ho!"

"Where away?" replied the captain.

"Dead ahead."

"What does she look like?"

' She is a piratical looking craft."

"Which way is she headed?"

"Towards Honolulu."

"We will give her chase."

We increased our speed, and when we were within twenty rods of her discovered that it was a native girl who had come out of a cross road. Our captain sang out: "Shake the reefs out of the topsails and sheet home the top gallant sails!" The captain of the craft ahead turned, looked back, put her hand to her face and waved us a challenge to come on, but she left us like the wind. She had a good sailing craft and was soon out of sight. As we rode into town it rained hard for about fifteen minutes, and made the roads very slippery. A Prussian sailor stopped his horse and said: "My craft gave a lee lurch and carried away one of my main shrouds. We will have to heave to, slack up the lanyards and put a shroud knot in the rigging." I soon fixed his stirrup strap.

We turned and rode up a valley into the mountains, and from an elevated point of vantage enjoyed a grand and comprehensive view of the country, the town and the harbor and shipping. We spent several hours very pleasantly, then about ship and started homeward bound, arriving in Honolulu about dark.

There was a large building in Honolulu named after the English frigate Blonde, fitted out with card tables, a bar at one end, and a small orchestra that furnished music night and day for sailors to dance. But you would find more young men of the town in the place at any time than sailors. Of course, some sailors resort to such places. Long voyages are monotonous, and they are bound to find some recreation when ashore. Some people think that all sailors invariably resort to the grog shop as soon as they get into port, but that is a mistaken and unjust conclusion. More than half of them are strictly temperate, never enter such places, deposit their money in savings banks, and many have several thousand dollars laid by. Others invariably spend their last dime. I remember one old tar who found nine cents in his pocket after we got out to sea. He held it in his hand, looked at it and said: "Dang my tarry top lights and top gallant eyebrows; why did I not spend that? I may chaw sand before I have another chance. I have no wife or children and it will be lost!"

A great many things are laid to sailors of which they are not guilty. They are fond of dancing the French four and telling stories, "spinning yarns," they call it. Some think the sailor has an easy time at sea, but that is a mistake. The ship is his home; he must keep everything in order; watch the elements, make or shorten sail and trim them to the winds. Beyond the ship nothing meets the eye but the mighty expanse of water. They are frank and free hearted, and their hands are ever open to assist others in distress. They are accustomed to hardships and danger, but the afflicted never appeal to them in vain for sympathy or succor. In these humane qualities, they compare favorably, as a class, with those who dwell on the land surrounded by all the comforts of life.

Catching the porpoise and sharks are popular pastimes. A large white bird, called the gonie, affords considerable amusement. It measures ten feet from tip to tip of wing, and has a habit of hovering about a ship when hove to during a gale. The sailors attach a large fish hook to a strong line, tie on a piece of wood to keep it afloat, bait the hook with a piece of meat and heave it out into the water. The bird swoops down and swallows the bait, hook and all. The men haul on the line and the bird, with outstretched neck, uses his large webbed feet and treads back with all his might. They pull him on deck, where he will stagger about like a drunken man, and fight with his captors, but cannot fly off of the deck. They skin the claws, tan them in alum water and make purses of them that will take in coins as large as a half dollar, easily. The wing bones are hollow and they make needle cases of them to sell in port. Of the fine white down of the body, they make pillows and bed spreads that are very nice and soft.

HOMEWARD BOUND

CHAPTER IX.

HOMEWARD BOUND.

The ship "Globe" and Capt. Benj. Price—Island of Juan Fernandez—The quinces and the jackass—Valparaiso and the Spanish Main—"Old Ironsides"—Tom Coleman and his parrot—"Doubling the Horn"—"Magellan Clouds"—Incidents of a gale—Storms at sea—"The White Squall"—Our stay at Rio de Janeiro—Arrive at Boston.

It was some time during the month of December that I shipped on board the ship Globe, of Boston, Capt. Benj. Price, master. She was homeward bound by way of the Spanish Main, and Cape Horn. She laid at Honolulu two or three weeks, and it was about the first of January, 1847, that we took our departure. We stopped at the island of Juan Fernandez, off the coast of Chili, to procure a supply of fresh water, as it is of better quality than can be found on the mainland. As we ran along the shore we could see large herds of goats of all colors feeding on the table lands. We hove the ship to, there being no harbor, rafted the casks and towed them ashore. A spout had been laid from a large spring to the sea, and by this means the casks were readily filled, then towed back to the ship and hoisted on board. Quinces were plentiful in the ravines and six of us, went ashore one day with pails to gather a quantity. The thickets were so dense that we could not see twenty feet in any direction. After a little I became separated from the others. I was busy picking and thinking how nice the quinces would be made into preserves with molasses, when all at once I heard an unearthly sound. I turned and ran down the ravine thinking all the animals in Africa were after me. I did not stop to choose my path, but tore through the bushes, lost my hat and all of my quinces, and came out with a scratched face. Two of the men saw me running and wanted to know were I was going. I replied: "To the ship. —Did you hear that noise?" "Yes; it was a jackass braying." I said: "It was worse than the rumbling sound of an earthquake, or the bellowing of a whale." They told me to go back and get my hat. I said: "I would not go back for a cargo of hats. If you want to stay and pick quinces you can. I am going to leave this desolate place. The quinces are sour." I went down towards the boat, ready to go aboard of the ship. I thought of what Selkirk said:

"I cannot hear the sweet music of speech,—
I start at the sound of my own."

That must have been before the importation of jackasses. I told one of the officers that the beast had good lungs but the tone of his voice was not very melodious, and rather harsh. I have heard the same kind of animal since but none to equal that one. It was some time before I heard the last of quince picking.

From Juan Fernandez, we sailed to the Spanish main, and stopped at Valparaiso. It was one of the toughest places I ever was in. Seventy-five sailors, called beach combers, were living there. They were rough fellows, and some of them kept *pulparees*, or as the Englishman spells it, "hess hay-hell-two hoes and a hen;" hell is the next thing to a *pulparee*.

The old frigate Constitution ("Old Ironsides") was on station there, and one of the crew, an old Irish sailor, by the name of Tom Coleman, owned a parrot that could talk. He came on board one night full of Spanish whiskey; the bird noticed it and sang out: "Tom Coleman, drunk!" Tom says: "What did you say?" The bird repeated: "Tom Coleman, drunk!" Tom picked up a piece of wood, struck the parrot and killed him. He did not intend to, and felt very bad when he realized what he had done in an angry moment. He sewed the bird up in a piece of canvass, buried him and mourned the loss of his pet.

It was in the month of June that we sailed out of the harbor and headed for Cape Horn. It was autumn in that latitude, and we had fine weather until we reached the latitude of southern Patagonia and Terra del Fuego. The weather grew gradually colder day by day. Strong west to southwest winds, accompanied by storms of snow and hail, gave us a heavy sea. We had the wind abaft the beam and the waves would break over the deck forward and amidship. Half hour tricks at the wheel were as long as a man could stand it without freezing. With close reefed main topsail and staysail, we held our course. The men stretched a rope from the mizzen mast to the main rigging, to hold to as they ran to and fro to keep from freezing. It was so cloudy for several days that we could not take an observation from the sun, and we ran farther south than necessary to clear the cape. When we got our bearings we found that we were in fifty-eight, south latitude. We were a happy lot of men when we squared the yards and headed the ship to the north. As she ploughed through the seas, the old tars would say: "The girls in Boston have hold of the towline and are hauling us towards home." We passed in sight of the Falkland Islands, and between them and the mainland. When we could see the north star we felt that we were nearly home. By this brief sketch of our experience while "doubling the Horn," you can see that a sailor's life is not all sunshine. Cape Horn is a terror to seamen,—they must be constantly on the lookout for icebergs, the cutwater and bobstays; each a mass of ice threatening destruction. It is not as pleasant as a good home on shore. At any time when the weather is clear, a light and a dark cloud, called the "Magellan Clouds," are to be seen hanging over the Straits of Magellan. I am unable to explain the cause of this singular phenomenon. I recollect that the officers had a theory in regard to it, but have forgotten what they said. Rows of penquins are seen sitting on the rocks, looking like soldiers arrayed for battle. If disturbed they dive under water.

When we were in the latitude of the La Platte River we spoke a Dutch galleyot, outward bound from Buenas Ayres, with a cargo of hides and tallow. They told us that the United States and Mexico were at war, and that we would have to look out for privateers. But when we arrived at Rio de Janeiro, we found it was a mistake, as Mexico had neither navy nor privateers.

After coming around Cape Horn we had strong winds; and as our ship was a good sailer by the wind, she was "wet" forward. Some vessels sail better with a free wind, owing to the peculiar model of the craft and the way the sails are set. The fast sailing vessel is more liable to be what the sailor calls "a wet ship," because she throws the sea and the wind blows the spray across the deck. You will hear a sailor ask these questions when shipping on a strange vessel: "Is she wet?" "Is it a good sea boat?" "Does she steer wild?" A fore and after or schooner will lie about four or five points off the wind and make fair headway; a square rigged ship about seven points.

I remember one night, it was after we were getting into better weather this side of the cape,—the wind was blowing fresh at eight o'clock in the evening when the starboard watch went below, leaving the first mate's watch, to which I belonged, until twelve, midnight. The wind increased, but the mate was a great man to carry sail, and would never give the order to shorten sail until he was obliged to for fear the masts might be carried away. We would hope to hear the order before the wind blew a gale, but as time passed and the wind increased we would rather he would "rag it to her" until the other watch was called. He would walk the quarter deck, casting his eyes aloft watching the sails, the men expecting every moment to hear the order: "Clew up topgallant sails!" But he would make his turn and back to the man at the wheel, while the old ship ploughed through the waves at a great rate, the water foaming under her bows and throwing the spray onto the forecastle deck. The sea was making the hissing sound, so familiar to sailors, like throwing a brand of fire into water. It seemed as though the ship wanted to fly, and we were anxious to hear eight bells. We knew that Dexter, the second mate, was an old "granny," as sailors call a timid or weak-kneed man, and would have his watch shorten sail as soon as he came on deck. The old ship was knocking the billows right and left, when the man at the wheel struck eight bells, and was quickly answered by the bell forward on the Samson's-post and the welcome sound for us: "Starboard watch, ahoy! Tumble up here, you sleepers, and let the wind blow your eyes open!" Then some old salt growled out: "Why don't you shorten sail?" They knew by the noise and thumping of the sea and the laboring of the ship that we were "ragging it to her," as the sailor calls carrying sail heavy. They knew how the first mate would carry sail, and said he did it to favor his watch. The other watch came on deck. We went below, stowed ourselves into our berths, laughing to ourselves because we anticipated that they would be ordered aloft immediately to shorten sail; and it was not long before we heard the order given: "Take in top gallant sails and haul down flying jib! Stow the sails snug so they will not blow out from under the gaskets." Then we could notice a difference in the motion of the vessel. She did not plunge or labor so hard. When we came on deck at four o'clock in the morning, the wind had abated and we soon had all sail on her again and were speeding away for Rio de Janeiro, Brazil.

There are several kinds of storms with which ships have to contend. The regular gale is not so bad as the monsoon, that terrible periodical wind of the Indian Ocean; the typhoon of the Chinese seas; or the white squall common to tropical latitudes. The regular gale comes on gradually and the mariner is notified of its approach in time to shorten sail and make everything secure. The waves rise higher than in the fierce squall, but follow one after another in regular succession, less dangerous than the contending currents of wind and swirling waves of sudden storms. But one must experience a storm at sea to fully comprehend the terrible aspects and dangers of the situation. The ship is battling for life against the wind and waves; the sea is awful in its wrath, and it seems every moment that the sailor's home must surely be engulfed in a watery grave.

The storm sails are close-reefed topsail and fore topmast

staysail, whether the ship be hove to, or scudding before the wind. Some ships cannot run before the wind because the masts would roll out of them. It is owing to the model, or because the bearings are not sufficient to prevent rolling, but they work all right when hove to.

The typhoon, Chinese Tae-fun, is a very dangerous storm. Its sudden appearance and strong rotary motion often dismast a ship before there is time to prepare to meet it. Fortunately, these storms are of short duration, and as the wind blows the sea down the waves are not heavy.

The white squall gives the shortest warning. It comes with terrible velocity, under a cloudless sky, but woe to the ship that lies in its path. We encountered one off the Brazil Banks. We were sailing along with a light breeze on our starboard quarter. A few light, fleecy clouds were in sight, but nothing that indicated a storm. It was about four o'clock in the afternoon and I was serving my trick at the wheel. The captain, walking the quarter deck, chanced to cast his eyes to windward and saw that the sea was white. He sang out: "Clew up and shorten sail as quick as possible!" To me he said: "Keep her off before the wind." But before we had time to make any preparation, the mizzen topsail was gone and the topgallant sails and royals blew out of the bolt ropes. and all was confusion in less time than it takes to tell the story. In twenty minutes it was dead calm, but we had work the rest of the day to clear the wreck. It seemed as though it would take the masts out of the ship.

THE WHITE SQUALL.

The sea was bright,—the bark rode well,—
  The breeze bore the tone of the vesper bell.
'Twas a gallant bark, with a crew as brave
  As ever launched on the heaving wave.
She shone in the light of declining day—
  Each sail was set, and each heart was gay.

She neared the land where beauty smiles,—
  The sunny shores of the Grecian Isles.—
All thought of home, and that welcome dear
  Which soon should greet each wanderer's ear.
In fancy they joined in the social throng,—
  In the festive dance—in the joyous song.

A white cloud flies through the azure sky!
  What means that wild, despairing cry?—
Farewell, vision scenes of home!—
  That cry is, "Help! help! help!" Where no help can come.—
The white squall rides on the surging wave,
  And the bark is engulfed in an ocean grave!

We ran along the coast of Brazil to Rio de Janeiro. The light house is situated on the port side as you enter the bay, and is provided with a revolving double light—red and white The city is about eight miles up the bay. There are two ports,—one near the entrance and one at quarantine. It is a land-locked harbor roomy enough to hold all the navies on the globe.

Our captain wanted to get near the docks before we came to anchor, so we would not have to move again. He directed us to lay the cable along the deck, and when they hailed us from the fort to lift it with our hooks and let it clank down on deck, to make them believe we were hauling the cable. We were nearly opposite the fort when the order came: "Let go your 'ankra'!" That is the way the Portugese pronounced it. "Shake up the chains!" said the captain. We were sailing right along, and the order, "Let go your 'ankra,'" was soon repeated, and emphasized a little later by the discharge of a blank cartridge. "Let go the anchor!" said the captain. That salute cost the ship two dollars.

The inhabitants are of Portugese descent, and were not a very interesting people at that time. We stayed there about four weeks,—painted the ship, received three thousand sacks of coffee and one hundred and seventy crates of oranges, and replenished our supply of water. The streets of the city are narrow, excepting the thoroughfares leading in from the country over which the coffee and other produce is hauled in. They were about a hundred years behind other nations in the way of improvements. The coffee was brought in sacks on carts so constructed that the axle turned with the wheels, and drawn by oxen,—a very primitive vehicle that made a fearful noise when in motion. The houses were low with tiled roofs, and devoid of beauty in architectural design. Negro slaves did all the heavy labor.

One of the finest fountains on the globe is situated in the palace square near the bay. The structure is square and is built of white marble, and the water is brought from the mountains. The water falls from four spouts, one on each side into a marble trough from whence the overflow runs into the bay.

We had liberty days ashore. Our old cook had some deal with a grocer, owing him about three dollars and agreed to send him a keg of slush or grease that comes off the meat. He did not send it according to contract. The Portugese said it was a Yankee trick and that the cook could not soft soap him again. We told the cook, and he filled a keg with salt water soft soap and sent it to him. The grocer was mad and said he would fix the cook if he caught him on shore again. But he did not catch him.

Sunday is the day of sport with the people. They indulge in cock fighting, displays of fireworks, etc., and show little respect for the Sabbath

At last our cargo was all stowed away and we were ready for sea. It was about the first of July that we sailed out of the harbor with a fair wind, homeward bound. The ship was soon breasting the waves of the broad Atlantic, and ready to battle with the storms once more. Rio de Janeiro is in about 24° south latitude, and we would soon be in the southeast trade winds that would waft us on until we reached the equatorial region of variable winds and frequent calms. A belt about fourteen degrees in width, seven on either side of the equator, called "horse" latitude by sailors, is peculiar in this respect. A dead calm may continue for a week or more, or light winds from every point of the compass may be experienced within an hour.

Formerly, it was the general practice on shipboard to serve each man a ration of grog regularly every day; and usually, an additional allowance after extra work, such as reefing topsails, etc. This practice has been discontinued. The change is a wise reform and a blessing to sailors. I was returning from the theater one night in New York. It was after midnight. I heard some one speaking in a basement, and out of curiosity, I went down the steps and entered the room, where I found an old white-haired sea captain delivering a temperance lecture in true sailor style, to an audience of fifteen or twenty old sailors. They listened attentively while he pictured the evils that result from the habit of drinking intoxicating liquors. After the lecture, every one of them made his mark after his name affixed to the pledge, and stated that heretofore they had never had a shot left in the locker after a bout in the grog shop, but that henceforth they would stow it away in a savings bank, and have something to help themselves with when they finally came to anchor on shore.

After crossing the equator we had a fine run as far as the Bermudas when we encountered some heavy rain squalls accompanied by thunder and lightning, that gave us some trouble. We were now engaged in taking off the chafing gears and otherwise putting the ship in fine shape for entering the harbor. We had some foggy days along our coast, when we would frequently hear the fog horns and meet small crafts. We hailed one, went on board of her and bought some water-melons and vegetables.

At the entrance to the bay we took a pilot and were soon at anchor in Boston harbor. It was the 19th day of August, 1847. As soon as we were alongside the dock, the boarding house sharks were after the sailors with their smiles and blarney, asking: "What house will you stop at? We have everything nice at the sailor's home. Have your morning tips before meals, good beds, and we will take your chests ashore." They take great interest in the sailor's welfare, planning to bleed him of his last cent before he goes to sea again.

You will see the sailor rolling along the sidewalk with his hands open as if to grasp a rope. He is ever ready to share his last dollar with his shipmates, and he never passes a beggar without giving him a dime, at least. They had a friend in Father Taylor, who was devoted to their interests and welfare. He warned them to shun places of vice, pointed the way to the Sailor's Bethel, and invited them to come. There was not a place on the globe where he was unknown to sailors, and universally regarded as their best friend; and they brought him the relics and curiosities they gathered during their voyages.

When we look at the hardships, sufferings and perils of the sailor's life, with its few enjoyments, let us remember with gratitude the service he renders to society. Consider that, through his courage and energy, we enjoy the many advantages of commerce, and the blessings of civilization and Christianity have been spread abroad. Therefore, let us hope that when he has made his last voyage and is broken down by age and toil, he may find a sunny harbor secure from storms and trouble, where he may happily and tranquilly await the inevitable summons aloft.

CHAPTER X.

THE MARINER'S LIFE.—ADVICE TO THE BOYS.

Perhaps some of you young men have an inclination to become mariners. As I experienced something of the inside working of a sailor's life while sailing round our globe, I can give you a little advice: Never leave a good home to go to sea. There are plenty of rough boys in the large seaports, lounging about the docks and wharves who make good seamen. They are acquainted with sailors and shipping, and are better fitted for that kind of business. A voyage at sea is a good schooling for bad boys. I once heard of a boy by the name of James Packard who was indicted for petty larceny. He was allowed to choose between going to prison or on board of a whale-ship. He chose the latter. His father told me some years later that James made a wise choice, as he became master of a ship, and a useful man. On the other hand if he had been sent to prison he might have become discouraged, thinking that everybody looked down on him, and ended by committing other crimes.

It is not every man that will make a good sailor. He must be alert and active,—able to think and act at the same time. He must have his mind on his work, especially when aloft, for sometimes there is great danger and occasions that require quick work.

I knew two young men of Shawano, who wished to become sailors. I will not mention names. They went as far as Chicago and shipped on board of a sailing vessel. One day they undertook to go up aloft. One succeeded in climbing up about twenty-five feet, and the other about fifteen.

At this point the one in advance chanced to look down; he became giddy-headed and said to the other: "I don't believe I will ever make a sailor. Let's go home to Shawano!" The other replied: "Have you got a good hold?" "Yes." And looking down at his shipmate, he found that he was hugging the rigging so close that he could hardly see him, and was gripping the shrouds so hard that the tar was oozing out between his fingers. He said: "I am going home as soon as I can get loose." Number one replied: "Oh! you will make a good sailor. A cyclone could not blow you off the rigging." "Oh, come on, let's go home!" They finally managed to get loose and descend to the deck. They counted their ready money and found that they lacked about three dollars of having money enough to pay their fare to Green Bay. They succeeded in getting work at unloading lumber and posts from a vessel, and made up the deficiency. At Green Bay, they took another invoice of their bank stock and found they had a balance of twenty cents in their favor. They concluded to "splice the main brace" and take the tow path to Shawano.

When they arrived at Bonduel, they were tired and hungry and stopped at the house of a hospitable old farmer by the name of Stern, and asked for bread and milk. After eating heartily, one of them thrust his hand deep into his pocket as if to pull out a full purse, when, in fact, it did not contain one penny. The old man said it was all right, that he did not charge them anything. That relieved them, and they trudged on towards home. But they concluded to come into the city by the pale light of the moon, for fear their shipmates at home would ask them what kind of a voyage they had made. They sneaked in by way of the alleys, stowed themselves away in their berths to dream of the experience they had had of a sailor's life. Their minds wandered back to the rolling deep, and between snores one burst forth:

"I am a little sailor boy.
 And would you know my story?
I've been across the ocean blue,
 And seen it in its glory.
I've seen it on a summer's day,
 As gentle as a child;
I've seen it in a tempest,
 Like a giant fierce and wild."

"Oh, stop that noise and go to sleep! You are no sailor; you don't know a windlass from an anchor."

Shortly he dreamed again:

"I've been in the ship
 When the waters were asleep,
She seemed like a rock
 Her steady place to keep.

I've been in the ship,
 When driven by a gale
She plowed the foaming billows
 With her sad, riven sail."

"Now, if you don't stop that howling I will never go to sea with you again. Do you think we are on the raging sea? We are in granny's bedroom. Now keep still. You will hear Mike Devlin call the morning watch pretty soon."

If you try it, you will find that the seamans life is fraught with hardship and danger. You will need lots of courage to make good sailors. Take my advice and stay on shore.

I will endeavor to give you some idea of the inside workings of a sailors life. An American protection is a document issued pursuant to the provisions of an act of Congress, passed for the relief and protection of American seamen. It bears the American eagle at the top, states your residence, name, age, weight, height, color of hair and eyes, complexion, etc. No sailor should neglect to obtain one before going to sea. It is invaluable in case sickness, accident, or any difficulty befalls you in a foreign land. Our government has a representative, called a consul, in every large seaport on the globe, and it is a part of his duty to relieve American seamen in distress, and settle differences between the men and officers of shipping. If a sailor has cause against an officer, he can make complaint to the consul and obtain redress. If sick, he will send you to the hospital, and when you have recovered he will assist you in getting another vessel. Every sailor is supposed to pay twenty cents per month out of his wages for the support of marine hospitals.

When you go on board of a ship that is ready for sea, you are chosen by an officer and become a member of his watch. The first mate heads the larboard watch, and the second mate the starboard, or Captain's watch. They are termed the starboard and larboard watches. Each watch has eight hours on deck, alternately, excepting the dog watches, as they are called, from four o'clock to six, and from six to eight P. M. This arrangement changes the time so that the same watch will not have to serve the same hours every night. In the watches, each man serves a two hour trick at the wheel and two hours as lookout, successively, in rotation.

The regular routine of a sailor's life at sea is to trim, or shorten sail, as required, and keep everything in order about the ship. The deck is scrubbed every morning with a broom designed for that purpose. They have a stone with ropes attached, called a holy stone. Two men draw it back and forth. This process is called holy stoning the deck. A smaller stone, called a prayer book by sailors, is used where the large one cannot touch. As there is no soil, or dirt, everything is tidy and clean. Swabs of ropeyarns are used to dry up the deck. They usually have plenty to do, working ship, making spun-yarn or marline, using the serving board, or mallet, and mending sails.

There are what is termed running rigging, and standing rigging. The shrouds, backstays, fore, main and mizzen mainstays, and the bobstays running from the cutwater to the bowsprit, constitute the standing rigging. The running rigging are the ropes used in making, reefing and taking in sail. The sailor has something to learn in this department, as only a few are called "ropes." Excepting the footropes, bucket and main ropes, they are called clewlines, buntlines, halyards, reef tackles, etc., etc. You are not a competent sailor until you know where all these ropes run, the blocks they pass through, the purpose and function of each, and the place where each comes through the fair leader and is belayed on deck. If you are called in a hurry some dark night to shorten sail, you must know what rigging to use, as there are no lights, except the binnacle light over the compass to see to steer by. And when you go aloft you need to know which is safe, as most of the rigging is not safe to hold onto when the ship is rolling and the wind blowing a gale. It requires plenty of nerve, quick work and strict obedience to orders in every instance, as everything depends on the activity and capability of the seamen. It is a good place for boys who disobey their parents, for when an order is given you cannot stop to ask questions, but must start instantly; not do like a boy I once heard of who did not know his duty. He was ordered aloft one dark night He said: "Captain, as for me going up this rope ladder this dark night without a lantern, I SHA'N'T DO IT!"

The officer of the watch grabbed a rope and went for him, saying: "Get up the rigging, you land lubber, or I'll cut you in two!" So you see you cannot stop to parley with them.

The bill of fare consists of duff, or what we would call a pudding. It is boiled in bags, and is usually served twice a week with salt pork, beef tea and coffee. One day they will have boiled rice for dinner, another day beans, and Friday is what is called "banyan day", when nothing but meat, crackers or sea-biscuit, tea and coffee is served. The cook hands it down into the forecastle in a measure something like a peck measure, called a "kid." Every sailor has a two-quart pan for his soup, a quart cup for his coffee, and a sheath knife to eat with Sometimes the beef looks hard and tough, and some old salt will look down into the kid, sorrowfully, and repeat the old saw:

"Old hoss, old hoss, how came you here?
Thou hast carted stone for many a year,
'Till killed by blows and sore abuse;
Then salted down for sailor's use.
The sailors, they do me despise;
They turn me o'er and damn my eyes;
They pick the meat from off my bones
And toss the rest to Davy Jones."

The naval laws compel captains to procure fresh provisions whenever practicable; and allow men twenty-four hours liberty whenever the ship enters a port, or once in six months. The regulations on ship-board are as steady as a watch in keeping time. Every man knows his duty and must obey orders strictly, at all times. Disobedience is mutiny, punishable with death.

The man at the wheel strikes a small bell every half hour, that is answered by a larger one forward on the sampson post. Four bells relieves the man at the wheel; eight bells ends a watch. One object in striking the bell at night is to know that the lookout is not asleep. The man at the wheel cannot go to sleep, because he must keep his eyes on the compass. They have two compasses, one for light and one for heavy weather. The latter will not traverse quick enough when the wind is light; and when the sea is heavy the light-weather needle will bob around so fast that it is impossible to steer by it.

I studied but one geography—Peter Parley's. From it I learned but one thing that I can remember. In describing the sea, the author says: "In a calm the sea is smooth, like the face of a mirror; but, 'oh! how dreadful in a storm!" I remembered that, and realized the truth of it whenever I saw old ocean in her wrath. Perhaps all sail is set when you turn in at eight o'clock, but the weather is "looking wild." When your watch is called at midnight, you hear the water thumping against the sides and the ship is rolling and pitching through heavy seas. When the companion-way is open you hear a dismal roar and the wind is howling through the rigging. You are in Egyptian darkness and hear the officers trumpeting their orders and the men shouting from aloft, as they reef the topsails. It is enough to terrorize any man. It was on such occasions as this that I would think: "Oh! how dreadful in a storm!" But the work must be done. If a man falls overboard, rescue is impossible. A boat would be smashed to atoms in a moment, and it is useless to throw anything out in the darkness. His grave is the sea, where thousands have found burial.

Spinning yarns is a favorite pastime. In every crew there is usually someone who can play the violin, or banjo, and the rest will dance from six o'clock until eight, evenings. The first dog watch, from four o'clock until six, is occupied in cleaning and sweeping the decks. At eight bells one watch goes below. The watches are changed at midnight, and again at four o'clock in the morning. From four o'clock until eight, A. M., is called the morning watch, and at its close all hands are called on deck to prepare for breakfast. Then one watch has the forenoon below. That is the way they put in their time at sea. Plenty to do every day in the week. There is an old saying that expresses it:

"Six days thou shalt work and do all thou art able.
Sundays, holy stone the deck and scrape the cable."

They usually do their washing Sundays. Practically there is no religious Sunday "off soundings." All days are alike to them

They are constantly on the lookout for other ships, and when one is sighted they run towards each other until within hailing distance, then use the speaking trumpet: "Hail! what ship is that? Where from and where bound?" She answers, and asks the same question. Other questions follow, then they steer so that each can read the name of the other on the stern. A boat will lower from each ship and the Captains, each accompanied by one of his officers, meet and exchange boat's crews. This constitutes the usual exchange of courtesies. They swap news, and occasionally someone gets a letter from home. This visiting at sea is called gamming. We spoke a ship off the coast of New Zealand, and learned that James K. Polk was president of the United States. He had been in office over a year. One old salt said: "It is good; if Pork is president we will get more pork than beef." He mistook the name. On shipboard, we usually get two barrels of beef to one of pork. A sail, or land looks good after months at sea.

The sailor takes pride in having his ship tidy, the rigging set up taut, and everything shipshape. When they enter port, the sails are furled nice and the bunts are smooth, for this attention to details denotes good seamanship. Old Jack tar is proud of his ship—his home.

A burial at sea is the most solemn occasion; and rugged old tars, who scorn all weakness in the face of danger, shed many a tear at the loss of a loved shipmate. The remains of the departed are sewed up in canvass, and a cannon ball, or bag of sand is attached to the feet. The ship is hove to, and the yards and rigging are creaking mournfully. The bier is a plank. Two men hold one end of it, and the other end rests on the rail amidship. On this plank the corpse is laid, with the feet to the sea. All hands are called to witness the burial. If there is no one to offer a prayer, they read one out of a prayer book. The first mate gives the word: "Launch!" and the dead man slides feet foremost into the sea. The sailors turn away looking sad, without saying a word. Then they brace around the yards and file away. You never hear a sailor mention the evil traits of the departed; when they speak of him, it is to recall his good qualities. They are very superstitious, and for a while are shy when going about the decks during a dark night; but it soon wears off and is foregotten.

Such is the life of a seaman. He is exposed to many hardships and dangers. A fall from aloft is quite sure to end his life, whether he strikes the deck or goes into the water. Two young English lads were furling the topgallant sail, and the seizing that held the foot rope parted. They fell overboard and that was the last that was seen of them. The ship was laying over so that they missed the deck, but either meant certain death. When I see boys who disobey their parents, I think it would be a good place for them on shipboard. There they soon learn that they must obey those in authority over them. It is worse for you if you refuse to obey any order of a superior, and there is no chance to skulk or run.

There is something fascinating in the sailors life. It is in seeing strange countries and people; and to many there is nothing more attractive than a ship under full sail. I think it is one of the finest sights I have ever seen. It is grand when passing another ship at sea; she rises majestically on the crest of a wave, and a moment later is lost to view in the trough of the sea.

I remember when I first started out on the whaler, and while crossing the gulf stream, we had to break out for water. We had to carry it in pails to the scuttle out on the quarter deck. It held ten or twelve barrels. I had been sick, was very weak, and not yet accustomed to the motion of the ship. The ship was rolling, and it was difficult for me to carry two pails of water without spilling some of it. Nevertheless, if you allow any to slop over you are called a land lubber and all sorts of pet names. It is not pleasant, but you have to stand it, and not say a word back; but get your sea legs on as soon as possible. I tell you, boys, you may think it nice, but you are likely to change your minds if you ever come to the actual experience. If you should go to sea, do the very best you can, or it will be the worse for you. If you try to shirk the officers will notice it, you will be set at all the extra jobs and hazed about the deck, until you feel that life is a burden. Do your level best on all occasions, without grumbling. It will pay you in the end.

When we sail out on the ocean, we are astonished at its immensity. On every hand it stretches away beyond the horizon, and there is no landmark to guide the mariner on its surface. And when we see its face agitated by storms, listen to the thunder of its billows, and meditate upon its uncertain and mysterious character and the dangers associated with it always, we are awed by the majesty of its presence. Familiarity does not diminish our appreciation of its power, its grandeur, or its sublimity. One can hardly realize its vast extent, until he has crossed the mighty waste of waters.

My work is finished. In the foregoing pages I have given a brief, but strictly truthful summary of my adventures during a few years of my early life. To matters of fact I might have added creations of fancy, and the result might have been a more readable book, for those who read for entertainment, only. But I have tabooed romance, preferring to submit simply a faithful transcript of events as they occurred. If I have thrown any light that will benefit the young, in trying to show them the dangers and perils of a seaman's life, I shall feel satisfied with the result of my effort in that direction.

FINIS.

CONTENTS.

CHAPTER I—FROM LAKE COUNTY TO THE EQUATOR............5

Opening scenes—A friend at Albany—The whaleship Margaret Scott—Capt. Plaskett, the "Old Horse"—The start from New Bedford—Making Marline—Purpoise fishing—Flying fish—Sailors' laws—Cape de Verde Islands—Capt. Plaskett has tremens—Crossing the equator—Neptune initiates a subject—Incidents and anecdotes.

CHAPTER II.—WHALE FISHING...17

Preparatory arrangements aboard ship—The pursuit and capture of leviathan—Dangers of the chase—Securing and stowing the oil and bone—Death of our first mate—St. Paul's Island—Captain and new mate have a row—Trouble between the captain and Dr. Winslow—Island of Toboai—Arrive at Tahiti.

CHAPTER III.—FAREWELL TO WHALING.......................31

The doctor gets even with the captain—Rum and bilge water—Deserting the ship—Exciting experiences—Meet shipmates—Visit the Windward Islands—Incidents of the trip—Return to Pata—French vs. natives—Battle of Point Venus—Missionary shot—Tahita—Characters and customs of the natives—Aboard the Shepherdess.

CHAPTER IV.—TRAFFIC WITH THE NATIVES..................41

The brig's equipment and business methods—Island of Rarotonga—We entertain visitors—The captain and the cannon—The Samoan group—How we lost our anchors—The Fijis a treacherous people—Girl offered for a musket—Remarkable differences in character—The Chain Islands—Taken sick and left on the Friendly Islands.

CHAPTER V.—LIFE AMONG THE NATIVES......................47

The old lady doctor—Primitive barbering—Lafa Lafa—An exciting experience—An object lesson—Learning the language—Go to Tonga—A native festival—Mr. Thomas, and his unregenerate charge—The bark Jane Eliza—The darkey steward again—News of the whaleship—Earthquakes—Go to Vavau—Interpreting—Choosing a tamai—Joseph Arnold—Work of the missions—Native characteristics, etc.

CHAPTER VI.—LIFE AMONG THE NATIVES.—*Continued*....56

The native dress—Manufactures; cloth, mats, etc.,—Cooking—Bread fruit—The cocoanut tree and fruit—Marriage ceremony—The feitoka or native cemetery—Turtle hunting—Rambles in the interior—The tabued grave—The missionary's goat—The vaka or native canoe.

CHAPTER VII.—LIFE AMONG THE NATIVES.—*Concluded*...67

Joe Arnold, pilot, and the missionary's cast off beaver hat—Piloting and interpreting—Joe's blacksmithing outfit—Our business flourishes—Chief Nafau, my tamai (father)—Sad fate of a young whaleman—Flogging a brutal punishment—A better way—Capt. Benj. Price of Boston—of the natives; their history, manners, customs, etc.—Capt. Bligh's estimate—Old Joe and Captain Clark—Natives of different groups compared·

CHAPTER VIII.—MY TRIP TO THE NORTH....................76

Bidding adieu to the Friendly islanders—Old Joe's lecture—Reflection, "The Mariner's Grave—Arrive at Petropaulovski—Furs and salmon—A trip into the country—A clam bake—The Kamtchatkan dog—Start for the Hawaiian Islands—We encounter a gale—Arrive at Honolulu—My seaman's permit—The Hawaiian group—Kamehameha III—Tars and Poe—The great volcanoes—Capt. Cook's monument—Meet an old friend—The boarding hoes-s and the milk bottles—A day on horseback—The "Blonde" dance houu—Sailor characteristics—Pastimes at sea—The gonie.

CHAPTER IX.—HOMEWARD BOUND...........................88

The ship "Globe" and Capt. Benj. Price—Island of Juan Fernandez—The quinces and the jackass—Valparaiso and the Spanish Main—"Old Ironsides"—Tom Coleman and his parrot—"Doubling the Horn"—"Magellan Clouds"—Incidents of a gale—Storms at sea—"The White Squall"—Our stay at Rio de Janeiro—Arrive at Boston.

CHAPTER X.—THE MARINER'S LIFE.—ADVICE TO THE BOYS..100